SOUTH-EAST BRITAIN
ETERNAL BATTLEGROUND

By the same author:

J.H. THOMAS: A LIFE FOR UNITY

OBJECTIVE EGYPT

THE FAREWELL YEARS: THE BUFFS, 1948-67

AMIENS 1918

THE REGIMENTS DEPART: A HISTORY OF THE BRITISH ARMY 1945-70

THE BUFFS (Famous Regiments series)

GOLDEN MILLER

DESTINATION DUNKIRK: THE STORY OF GORT'S ARMY

THE QUEEN'S OWN BUFFS, THE ROYAL KENT REGIMENT

THE PLAIN COOK AND THE GREAT SHOWMAN: FIRST AND EIGHTH ARMIES IN NORTH AFRICA

THE MIDDLESEX REGIMENT

ALEXANDER'S GENERALS: THE ITALIAN CAMPAIGN 1944-45

To My Constant Assistants

Lucy and Elizabeth

SOUTH-EAST BRITAIN
ETERNAL BATTLEGROUND

by

Gregory Blaxland

With Sketches by the Author

MERESBOROUGH BOOKS
1981

Published by Meresborough Books, 7 Station Road, Rainham, Kent.
ME8 7RS.

ISBN 0 905270 444

Printed and bound by Mackays of Chatham

CONTENTS

MAPS

REFERENCES

The above show places named. Their Ordnance Survey map references are as a rule given in the text, and as a guide to accessibility ownership is indicated by use of letters as follows:

- DoE – maintained as an ancient monument by the Department of Environment and regularly open to the public.
- NT – National Trust property usually open to the public.
- DC – owned by the local District Council and usually open to the public.
- MoD – Ministry of Defence property, usually closed to the public, but access may be obtainable on application to the public relations officer at the nearest headquarters, as listed under Army or Navy in the telephone directory.
- PO – property Privately owned but Open to the public on at least two days a week during the summer months.

Thus Eynsford Castle (TQ 5465 – DoE) is to be found in 100-kilometre square TQ and in kilometre square of eastings 54 and northings 65 and is an ancient monument maintained by the Department of Environment and therefore regularly open to the public.

ACKNOWLEDGEMENTS

Being nearest the mainland of Europe, the people of the South-East have always been the most closely involved in the defence of Britain. I attempt in this book to describe the battles fought on their territory, the defences they have built, the internal conflicts in which they have been involved, and the contribution they have themselves made to the armed strength of the nation in peacetime and at war. The story begins before Caesar and ends after Hitler. I have confined it within the artificial frontier drawn by county boundaries while recognising the indivisible nature of national defence. My counties are Kent, Sussex, Surrey, Middlesex, and the prime objective of every invader, London.

I have grabbed information wherever I could find it, and the best of it has come from examination of the battlefields and of the fortifications by which Britons of all ages, Ancient and Modern, of Belgic, Roman, Saxon, or Norman origin, under the rule of Tudors, the reign of Stuarts, or the leadership of Pitt, Palmerston, or Churchill, have revealed their fears, their intentions, and their capabilities. I have received kind and enthusiastic help from a large number of people, and I am especially grateful to those who could provide both information and advice on the reliability of sources. They include Dr Frank Jenkins, of the Kent Archaeological Society, and Mr Simon Garrett, of the Sussex Archaeological Society; Mr F.W. Holling and Mr Matthew Alexander, of Guildford Museum; students of Dover's history in Mr Douglas Welby, Mr John Greenstreet, Mrs Sylvia Corrall, Mrs Sarah Campbell, and the expert in Coastal Gunnery, Colonel Bunny Arnold; Miss Anne Roper, historian of the Romney Marsh; Mr G.E. Trimblett, of Sheppey; Mrs Linda Piercy and Mrs Eileen Chapman, of Dorking's library, who obtained most useful information about the fictitious battle for Dorking and its consequences; Mr Tom Pearse, the Royal Navy's Public Relations Officer, Chatham; and the Royal Navy's representative in the debate on Operation Sea Lion, Rear Admiral Edward Gueritz.

Handbooks on local history, of which I acquired forty-one, have been of enormous value. They include a comprehensive list of Kent's Defences, compiled by Kent Defence Research Group, of the Archaeological Society, and publications issued by the two Sussex County Councils, entitled *The Fortifications of East Sussex* and *Archaeology in West Sussex: A Field Guide.* Scholars appointed by the Environment Department have produced admirable works on Dover, Deal, Richborough, Rochester, Upnor, Eynsford, and Farnham Castles, on the Saxon Shore Forts and the Tower of London. Of historical guides issued by local authorities I have gleaned most from those on Chichester, Hastings, Lewes, Winchelsea, Rye, Sandwich, and (for its part in the evacuation from Dunkirk)

Margate. For information on establishments owned by the Government I am particularly grateful to representatives of the Royal Artillery Institution, the Institution of Royal Engineers, Headquarters London District, The Queen's Regiment, Guards Depot, Staff College Camberley, RMA Sandhurst, Royal Naval College Greenwich, HM Dockyards Chatham, and Royal Small Arms Factory Enfield, also to the Keeper of Public Records for access to the war diary of the South-East's guardian in 1940, 12th Corps.

I am greatly indebted to the librarians of Canterbury and the Royal United Service Institute for providing all the books that have formed the backbone of my story. I have listed the chief of them in the Appendix, Books Consulted. For background information and atmosphere I have leant heavily on Winston Churchill's *A History of the English-Speaking Peoples,* and I am grateful to its publishers, Cassell and Company, for their kind permission to reproduce an extract.

GENERAL MAPS

South-East England

The Medway Defences

Dover's Defences

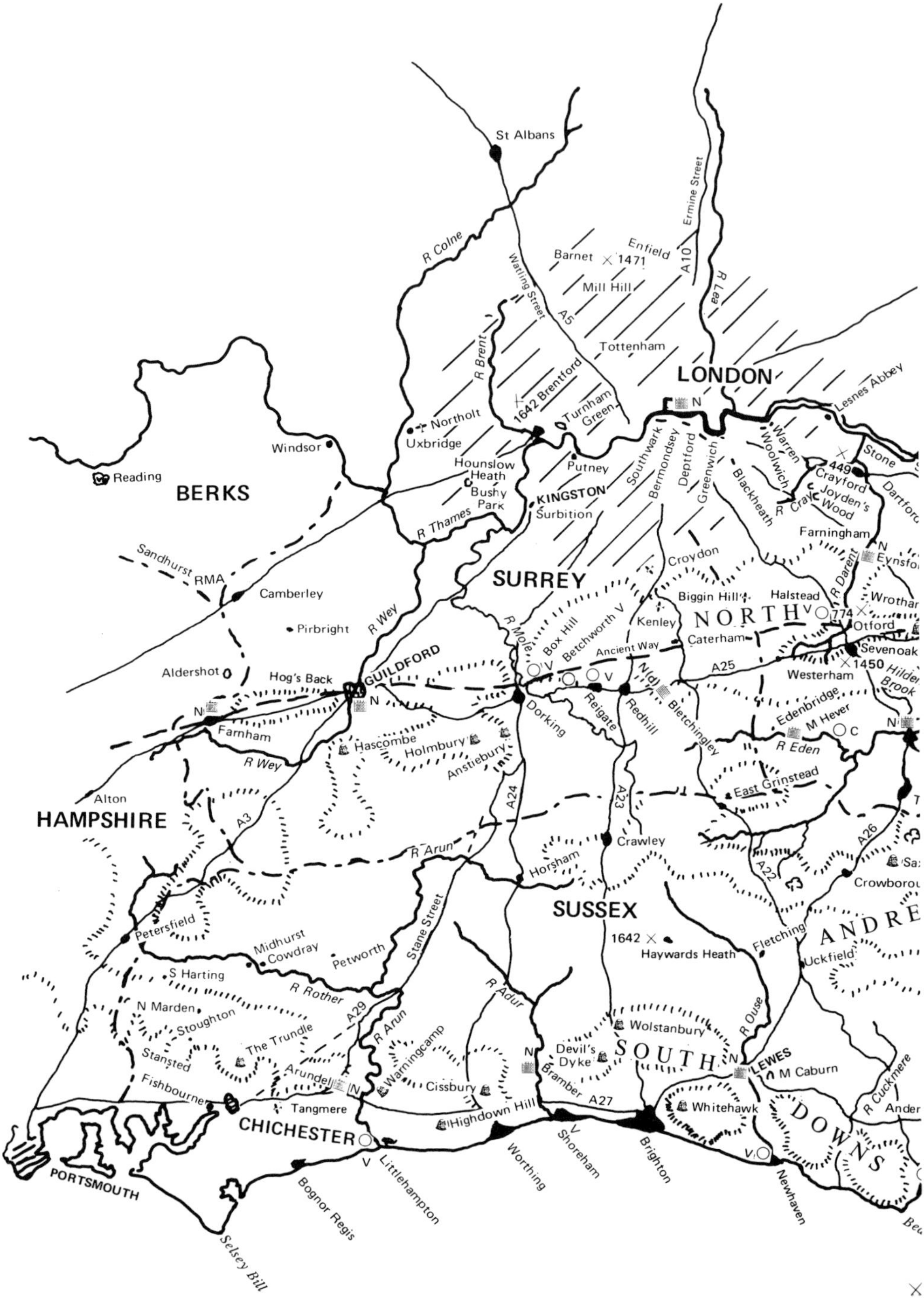
St Albans
Ermine Street
Enfield
Barnet
1471
A10
R Lea
Watling Street
Mill Hill
A5
R Colne
Tottenham
LONDON
R Brent
1642 Brentford
Turnham Green
Lesnes Abbey
Northolt
Uxbridge
Windsor
Reading
BERKS
Hounslow Heath
Bushy Park
Putney
KINGSTON
Surbition
Southwark
Bermondsey
Deptford
Greenwich
Woolwich
Warren
Blackheath
449
Crayford
Stone
Dartford
R Cray
Joyden's Wood
Farningham
Eynsford
R Thames
Sandhurst
RMA
Camberley
SURREY
Croydon
Biggin Hill
Halstead
R Darent
Wrotham
NORTH
774
Otford
Kenley
Caterham
Sevenoaks
Pirbright
R Wey
R Mole
Box Hill
Betchworth V
Ancient Way
1450
Westerham
Hilden Brook
Aldershot
Hog's Back
GUILDFORD
N
V
A25
Edenbridge
M Hever
C
Farnham
Dorking
Reigate
Redhill
Bletchingley
R Eden
Hascombe
Holmbury
Anstiebury
R Wey
Alton
HAMPSHIRE
A3
A24
A23
East Grinstead
A26
Crawley
R Arun
Horsham
A22
Crowborough
Petersfield
SUSSEX
Stane Street
1642
Haywards Heath
Fletching
ANDRE
Uckfield
Midhurst
Cowdray
Petworth
S Harting
R Rother
N Marden
Stoughton
A29
R Adur
R Ouse
Wolstanbury
The Trundle
R Arun
Warningcamp
Stansted
Devil's Dyke
SOUTH
LEWES
M Caburn
R Cuckmere
Arundel
Cissbury
Bramber
A27
Fishbourne
Tangmere
Highdown Hill
Whitehawk
DOWNS
CHICHESTER
Shoreham
Brighton
PORTSMOUTH
Littlehampton
Worthing
Newhaven
Bognor Regis
Selsey Bill

SOUTH-EAST BRITAIN

Symbols:

- Hillfort
- Castle, with period of origin denoted as follows:
  - R Roman
  - N Norman
  - M Medieval
  - T Tudor
- ○ Fort, Tower, Redoubt, Pillbox, or group of same, with origin denoted:
  - G Georgian (usually anti-Napoleon)
  - V Victorian
  - C Churchillian (World War II)
  - (d) when added to any of the above means destroyed but ruins visible
- original member of Cinque Ports and Ancient Towns
- Fighter Aerodrome of World War I or II (may no longer exist)
- × Site of Battle with date
- ·—· Inter-County boundary

Only old established roads are marked.

Contour marking at 300 metres.

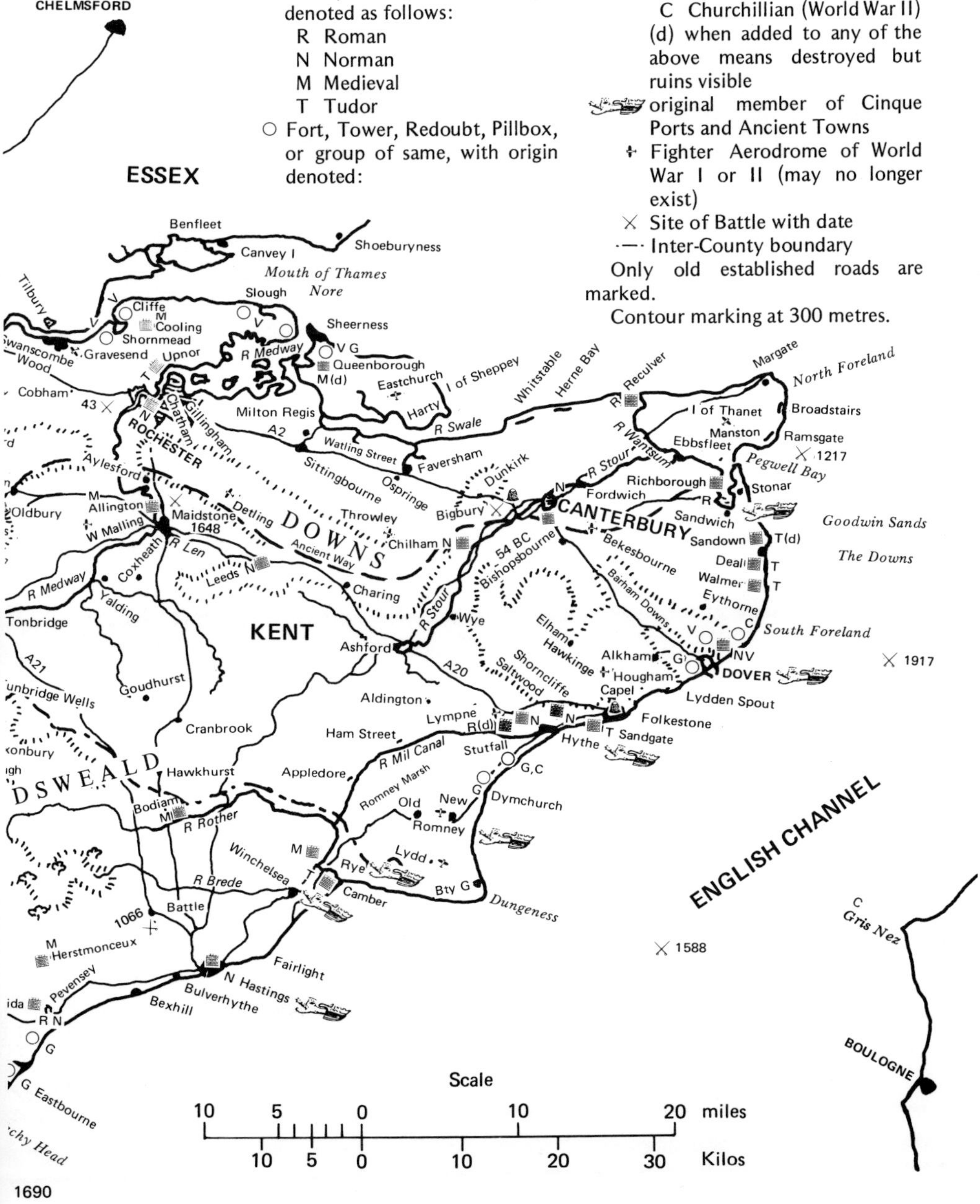

1690

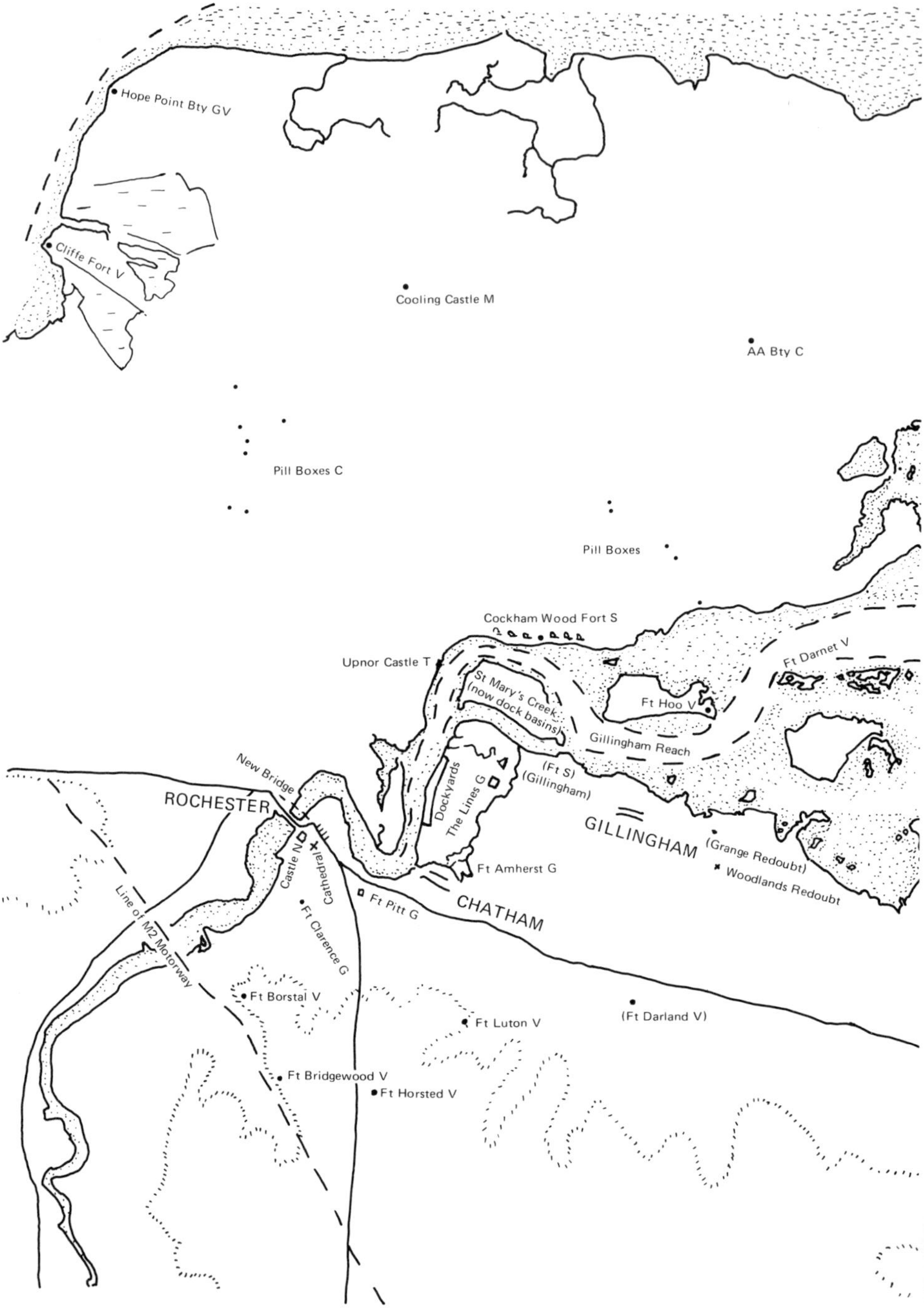
Hope Point Bty GV
Cliffe Fort V
Cooling Castle M
AA Bty C
Pill Boxes C
Pill Boxes
Cockham Wood Fort S
Upnor Castle T
Ft Darnet V
St Mary's Creek (now dock basins)
Ft Hoo V
Gillingham Reach
New Bridge
ROCHESTER
Dockyards
The Lines G
(Ft S)
(Gillingham)
GILLINGHAM
(Grange Redoubt)
Woodlands Redoubt
Castle N
Cathedral
Ft Amherst G
Ft Pitt G
CHATHAM
Line of M2 Motorway
Ft Clarence G
Ft Borstal V
Ft Luton V
(Ft Darland V)
Ft Bridgewood V
Ft Horsted V

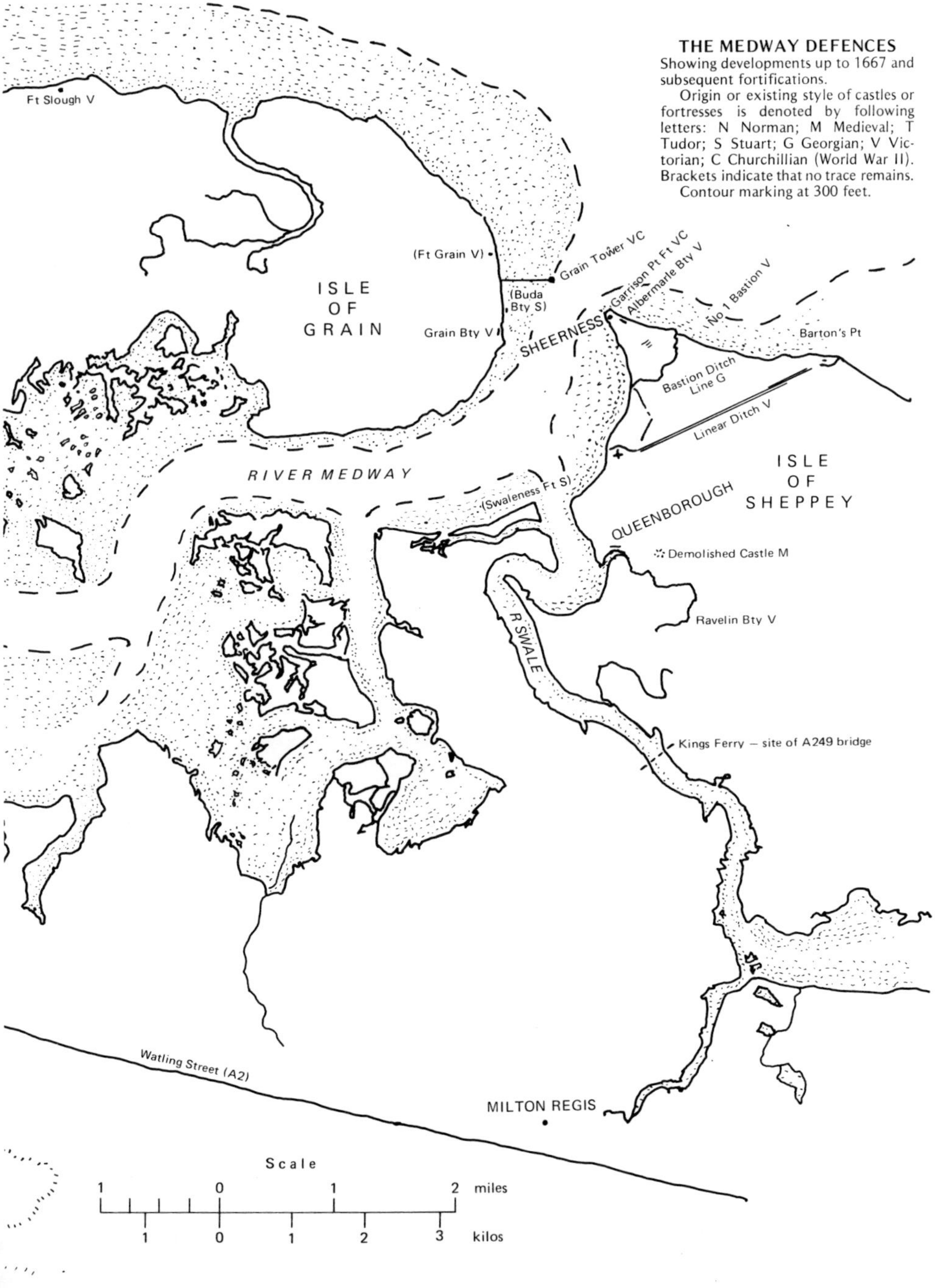

THE MEDWAY DEFENCES

Showing developments up to 1667 and subsequent fortifications.

Origin or existing style of castles or fortresses is denoted by following letters: N Norman; M Medieval; T Tudor; S Stuart; G Georgian; V Victorian; C Churchillian (World War II). Brackets indicate that no trace remains.

Contour marking at 300 feet.

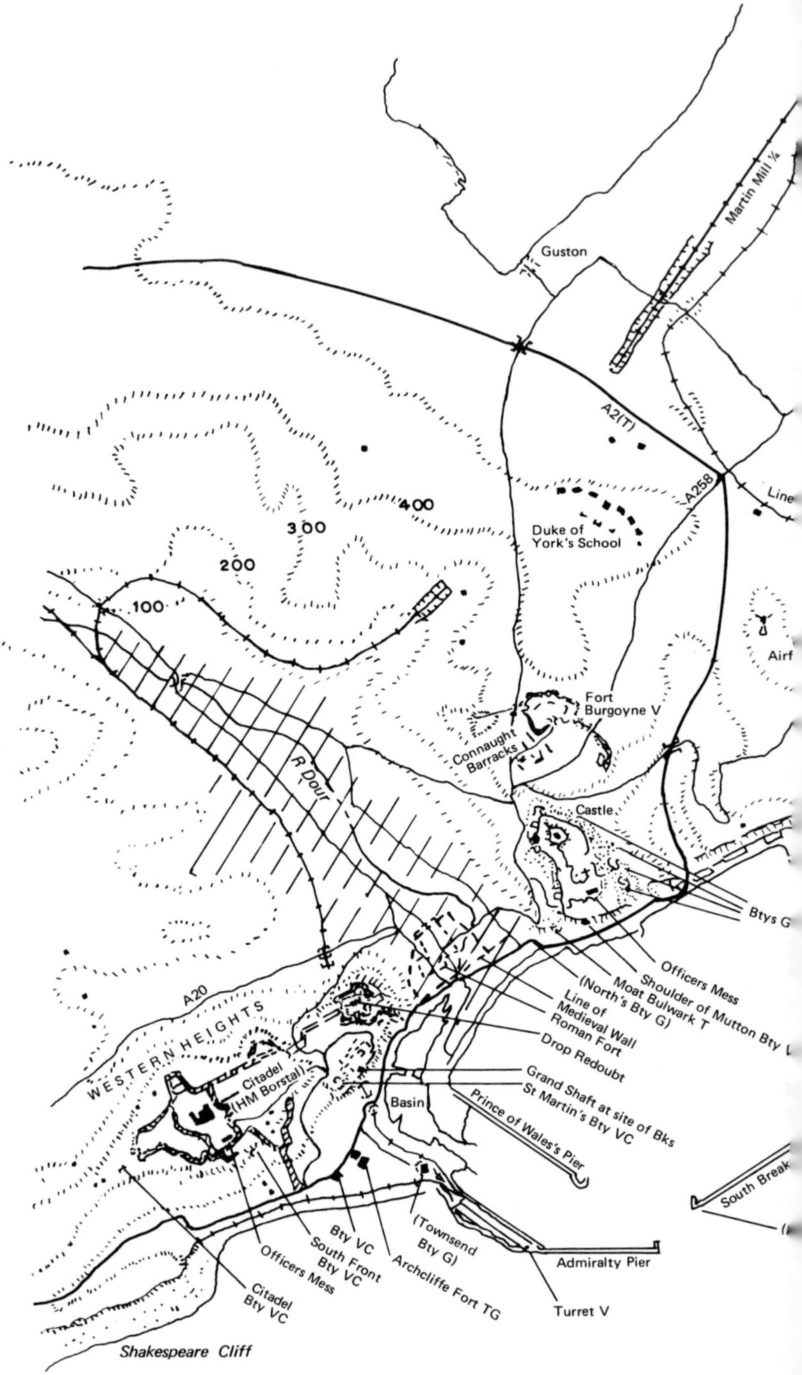
Martin Mill ¼
Guston
A2(T)
A258
Line
400
300
200
100
Duke of York's School
Airf
Fort Burgoyne V
Connaught Barracks
R Dour
Castle
Btys G
Officers Mess
Shoulder of Mutton Bty V
Moat Bulwark T
(North's Bty G)
Line of Medieval Wall
Roman Fort
Drop Redoubt
Grand Shaft at site of Bks
St Martin's Bty VC
Prince of Wales's Pier
South Break
A20
WESTERN HEIGHTS
Citadel (HM Borstal)
Basin
Bty VC
South Front Bty VC
Officers Mess
Citadel Bty VC
(Townsend Bty G)
Archcliffe Fort TG
Admiralty Pier
Turret V
Shakespeare Cliff

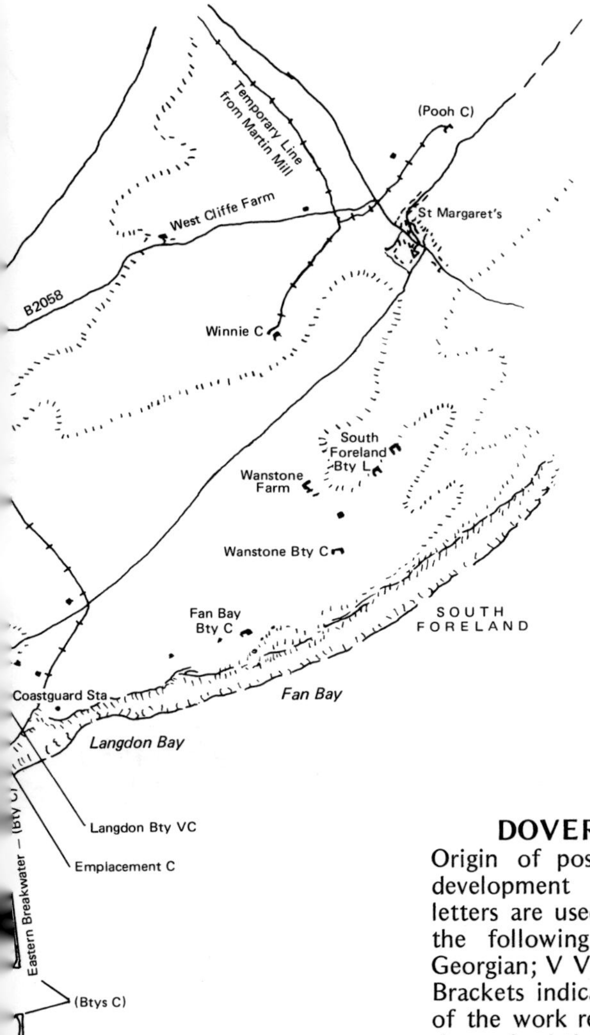

DOVER'S DEFENCES

Origin of positions, and subsequent development where two or more letters are used, are shown by use of the following letters: T Tudor; G Georgian; V Victorian; C Churchillian. Brackets indicate that no visible trace of the work remains. Dots mark positions of existing pillboxes.

Contour markings are at intervals of 100 feet.

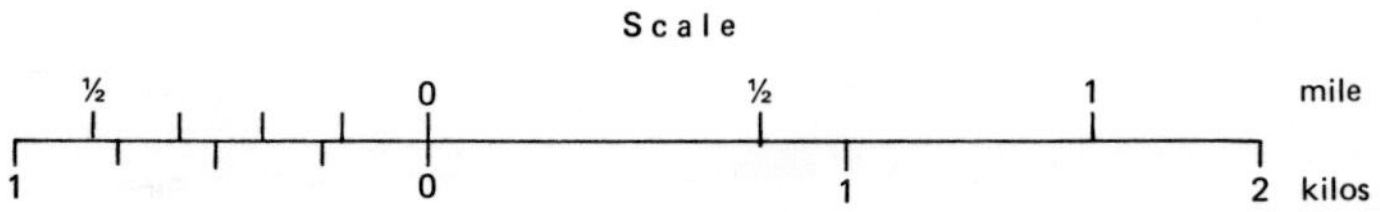

The Trundle

Chapter 1

THE HILLFORTS

The isthmus connecting Britain with the mainland of Europe is believed to have collapsed in some year around 6,000 BC, leaving two jagged white cliffs to glare their defiance at each other from a distance that was to expand to a minimum of 21 miles. This gave the people of Europe a new place of refuge or of discovery, according to inclination, and it would appear that those who came by the shortest route, in their driblets over the centuries, usually sought refuge from more warlike tribes, whereas those who landed on the western shores were of a more adventurous nature, coming from the sunnier coast of Spain or Britanny, where sailing had greater allure. Certainly more iron weapons have been excavated in Wales and the West Country, including the distinctive British dagger, which came into production in the 6th Century BC, by methods clearly copied from the Continent. It was used in tribal fighting, not for the possession of the island as a whole but for very small portions of it.

It is clear that the South Downs of Sussex have a longer history of savage dispute than any other part of the South-East, for they contain some remarkable specimens of early fortification. Being free of forest and swamp, the hilltops were of course both defensible and habitable, and palisades could have the dual function of keeping out raiders and keeping in livestock. Examination of Whitehawk Camp (TQ 330045, at the summit of Brighton Racecourse) has shown that even in the Neolithic Age, around 3,000 BC, use was made of wood to form a ditch and bank rampart round the hilltop. With the use of copper (from around 2,500 BC), bronze (2,000 BC), and iron (650 BC) defence works progressed very slowly from the earthen box formed by double rows of upright posts to the ditch and palisade perimeter behind which defenders could stand on a platform made by the use of a lower, inner row of posts. The development of weapons, domestic utensils, and living quarters did not lag behind that of defence works.

Many hills bear mark of the huge ditches dug around their summits, testifying both to the industry of those who scooped out the earth and built the ramparts and to the harsh experience of assault that brought realisation of the need. The Trundle (SU 8711), which overlooks Goodwood Racecourse, provides one of the finest examples, although tarnished by the modern masts and huts that stand within its ramparts. Since it dominates the country for miles around, its defences must have been in steady process of development for centuries before the completion, around 200 BC, of the easily visible ditch and embankment that encloses 12½ acres in octagonal shape at a maximum width of some 250 yards from gate to gate. The gates were the most vulnerable part of a hillfort, and these have inverted entrance passages upon which the attackers could be pelted with missiles from over the palisades above them on both sides. Remains prove that alterations became necessary, that the passages were made longer and the gates themselves ever more massive. Each had a large guardhouse near it, and two more ditches had to be crossed before the summit could be reached.

Seventeen miles to the east of the Trundle stands another marvel of ancient industry: the sheer-sided hillfort of Cissbury (TQ 1408 – NT). It has a rampart wall 30 feet wide, built in about 250 BC, enclosing a plateau of 60 acres, and it has been estimated that 9,000 tree trunks must have been used as revetment for the outer rampart. A huge force would have been needed to man the perimeter, and it would presumably have been formed by the summons of all tribal members, with their flocks and womenfolk, from the surrounding country. Another smaller fort overlooks the sea 3½ miles south-west of Cissbury, that of Highdown Hill (0904 – NT). The defences here are thought to date from 500 BC and, as on so many hilltops, they have received their periodic additions. The most conspicuous of the ruins on the summit are not in fact Roman, as might be thought, but the remains of army huts built in 1940.

As is indicated on the Ordnance Survey's special sheet for Ancient Britain, practically every peak on the Downs above Brighton was prepared for defence. Of special interest are the massive bank and ditch, and superb position, of the Devil's Dyke (2511), and the combination of the rampart and inner ditch around Wolstonbury (2813). Further eastwards stands the peak commanding access to the Downs and the River Ouse, and it will be seen to be worthy of its name of Mount Caburn (4408). The rampart here stands 20 feet above a wide flat-bottomed ditch and is of later date than the more westerly hillforts, having been built in haste probably through fear of the new invaders coming from the east. It encloses only a small area, which nevertheless contains the remains of 140 grain storage pits.

North of the Downs, running obliquely almost from the Trundle to join the coast to the east of Beachy Head, was the border of the great forest that was to take the name, from Roman-Saxon usage, of Andredsweald. It stretched 120 miles from west to east and (at most) 30 from south to north and, growing out of deep clay, formed an impenetrable barrier between the people of Sussex and Kent. However, there were deposits of iron ore under the clay, and as is shown by the overgrown remains of a mining fort at Saxonbury (5732), the Britons of the late Iron Age had begun to extract it. Well over a thousand years were to pass before the Weald began to be developed agriculturally, thus making the name synonymous with fertility in place of its original meaning, a wilderness.

Yet further inland the curving line of the North Downs formed the one means of communication across southern England, separating the swamps on the northern border of the Andredsweald from those of the Thames valley and connecting two stretches of downland below which lay hollows that were to be converted into bastions of religion, Winchester and Canterbury. Near its western extremity the range extends southwards, and three fine hillforts stand on this flank, as if guardians against raids from the South Downs: Hascombe (TQ 004386), Holmbury (104430), and Anstiebury Camp (153440).

The trackway linking west with east runs along the side of the North Downs, more often than along its summit, (as shown on map on pp 12-13) and it had been in use probably for more than two thousand years before it acquired the name of Pilgrims' Way. It formed the trade route with the Continent and gave access to and from the harbour of Richborough (TR 3259), due east of Canterbury. The development of Dover had to await the arrival of the Romans.

About the year 100 BC the Belgae invaded East Kent, probably more by tribal families than in a single coordinated horde. Like invaders of more westerly parts of Britain, they were of Celtic stock, and they came from roughly where Belgium is today. Their coins, instruments, and pottery testify to their culture, and as the Romans were to discover, they had also studied the art of war. They appear to have encountered little resistance. Although such obvious prominences as Castle Hill above Folkestone (2137) may have had their defences, there was nothing on the scale of the massive ramparts on the Sussex Downs. While developing the agricultural capacity of the Downs by the coast, the Belgae established their main camp, or fortified town, on a captured hillfort astride the main trackway, covering the crossing over the River Stour, which was wider than today. This was at Bigbury (1157), two miles to the west of the site of Canterbury. More will be said about it in the next chapter.

Further westwards in Kent, another large encampment has been located on the trackway, covering the point where it crossed some gault clay. This is named Oldbury (TQ 581561 – NT) and, through its woodland covering, defence works stretching almost a mile from south to north can be observed. It was a hillfort of natural strength, admirably situated both tactically and strategically, and although its ditch and rampart are meagre when compared with Cissbury or the Trundle, there is evidence that sufficient men were mustered here to repel an attack, probably made by the Belgae in their expansion from the east. They were now to receive further rebuff.

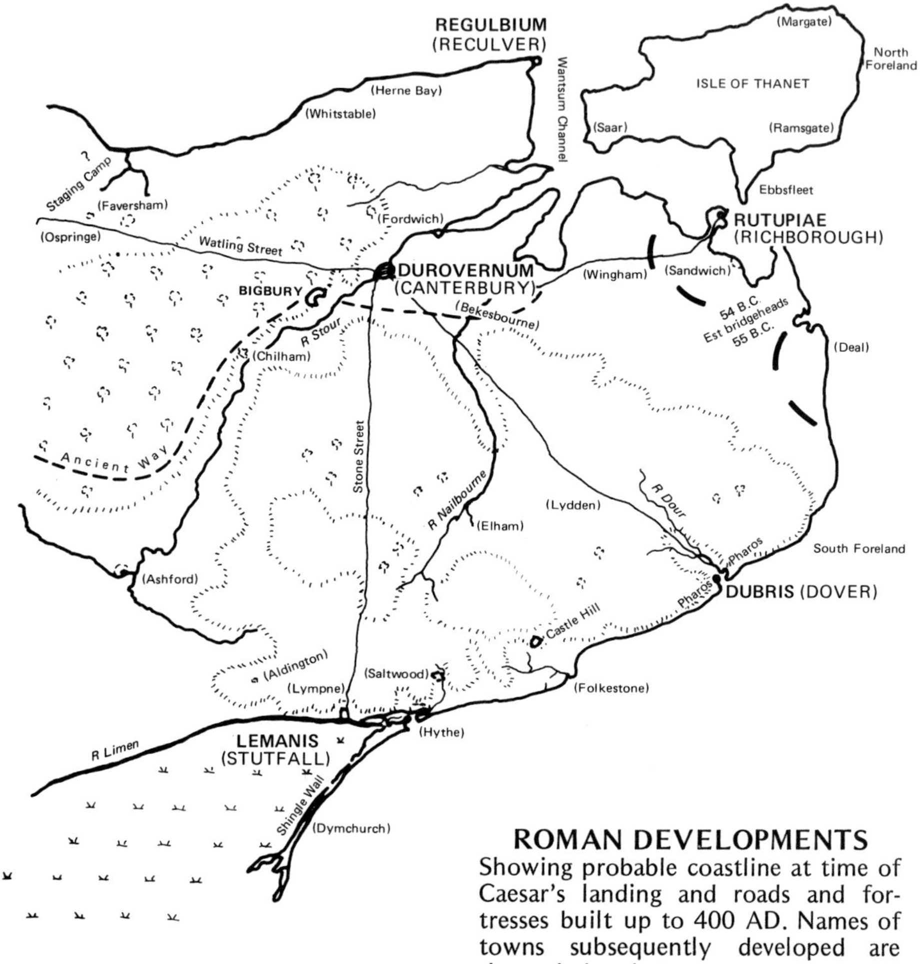

ROMAN DEVELOPMENTS

Showing probable coastline at time of Caesar's landing and roads and fortresses built up to 400 AD. Names of towns subsequently developed are shown in brackets.

Gradient lines at 200 and 500 feet.

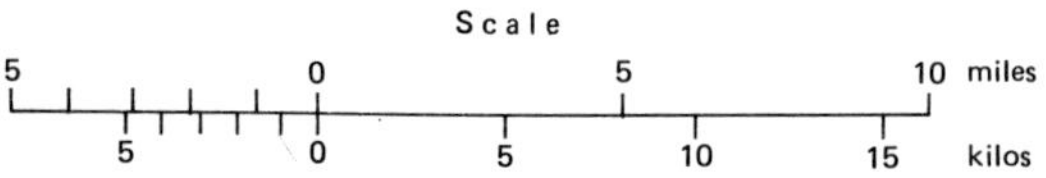

Chapter 2

CAESAR'S INVASIONS

In 55 BC the obscurity shrouding illiterate Britain was pierced by the pen of the first writing general, Julius Caesar, the Roman governor of Gaul. The account he has left provides of course only one man's view, and since he knew no place-names, except Cantium for Kent, the route he took presents a classic puzzle, which has in parts been converted virtually to certainty by modern detectives. Because he wrote for instruction, as much as for publicity, his work has a clear ring of accuracy – but no general will ever minimise the opposition he encounters, and it is therefore impossible to tell just how hard the fighting was.

It was outside Caesar's brief to occupy Britain and he planned nothing more than a raid, partly to intimidate the tribes who were giving aid and refuge to rebels against the Roman subjugation of Gaul, partly in response to the sheer challenge the venture presented. The Romans were for the most part landlubbers, and even though Britain could be seen from the coast of Gaul, they regarded it with awe, as lying beyond the Ocean, the far extremity of the world. However, they had gained command of the sea by their crushing naval victory over the Veneti (from Britanny) in 56 BC, and in the belief that the Britons could be won over merely by the threat of his coming, Caesar sent across an envoy in the person of an Atrebatic chieftain named Commius, thus showing how little he knew about the Belgic occupants of Kent. Commius was at once arrested.

Caesar went ahead with his plans undeterred. He had assembled two trusted legions for the assault role, numbered VII and X, and if they had been up to establishment strength, which neither was, each would have mustered 5,210 stormtroopers, which was some 500 more than the intended bayonet strength (also never fully achieved) of a British infantry division in the Second World War. Like the British infantry, the Roman organisation devolved into sections of eight men apiece, each armed with the broad, short sword and two javelins. He carried a shield, shaped to cover his trunk and made of wood with leather cover and metal binding, and wore a helmet adorned with crest, jointed body armour, and boots secured by binding round the calves. There were ten sections in a century, and six centuries in a cohort, except for the first cohort of each legion, which had five centuries of double strength. This large cohort was the first of ten.

For fire support, either from bows, slings, or from artillery, which hurled spears or stones by means of a giant catapult, Caesar relied on foreign mercenaries, the Auxilia. He put them into galleys of light draught, which could be manoeuvred at speed by their oarsmen, and he crammed his legions into eighty cumbersome transports, which had not been designed for an assault landing; each must have carried upwards of a hundred men. A force of 500 cavalry also came under orders to sail, but because there had already been so many delays Caesar ordered the main expedition to sail from Boulogne while the eighteen ships earmarked for the cavalry were still struggling towards the rendezvous. He duly set off across the Channel in the very early hours of August 26, 55 BC, travelling himself in a fast cutter.

By 9 a.m. he had a close view of the white cliffs of Dover, which probably looked much as they do today and were topped by the same green and open downland. He could not in fact see much grass, for it was covered by a mass of armed, animated, and in many cases mounted men; the enemy had been forewarned of his coming and were obviously in no mood to negotiate. It would be unwise to land immediately below them, and Caesar opted to continue the voyage 5½ miles further northwards, where his scouts told him that the cliffs subsided to some level flats. Not until 3 p.m. did the transports creep within lee of the white cliffs but now the wind blew in their favour and they took only an hour to reach the point of the cliffs' final descent (about 373504). Led by the horsemen, the Britons kept them in sight by running up and down the folds of the downland.

The boats must have stood off what is now the town of Deal, home of those specialists in amphibious warfare, the Royal Marines, and possessor of a magnificent squat fortress, which was built by King Henry VIII in the belief that this stretch of beach might again attract invaders. Although to the north the sea made greater inroads than today, the beach at Deal may have followed much the same line, leaving aside the present accumulation of shingle. It can be seen that the shingle descends sharply in steps or shelves, and certainly the Romans encountered this feature of the coastline and were greatly disconcerted by it, for the bows of the transports wedged themselves into the shelf, leaving the remainder of the boat in deep water. Since the upward curve of the bows made this the hardest part from which to disembark, any attempt at assault seemed likely to end in drowning. The longer the landlubbing, heavily armoured soldiers examined the prospect, the less they liked it.

Nor did the sight of the enemy on the beach rouse them to heroics. The Britons were long-haired, moustachioed men, with bodies daubed all over with blue woad, which (as observed by Caesar) 'gives them a more terrifying appearance in battle'. Some were in little chariots, which had become obsolete as vehicles of war in Gaul, and some rode ponies, and all showed great agility as they dashed in and out of the sea, hurling javelins, slinging pebbles, and making the Romans feel woefully heavily-laden and immobile. Caesar said (without specific reference to charioteers) that they 'spurred on their horses, which were trained to it' and he thereby sowed the seeds of the legend that the chariots made gallant charges through the surf.

It seems that at this stage there was nothing to charge. The sea-tossed Romans were stupefied into inactivity, and so they might have remained if Caesar had not made use of his galleys to bring his archers and artillerymen to within close range of the Britons' right flank. The shock of coming under fire from these mysterious weapons, which were quite beyond their ken, sent a palpable current of panic through them, on perceiving which the standard bearer of Legio X was inspired to take the plunge. 'Follow or betray your Eagle!' he yelled, in water up to his chest.

It was a lead that could not be ignored. There was a widespread splashing as the soldiers jumped overboard one by one and anxiously looked around for their centurions. The Britons rallied and made repeated attacks through the water with their javelins and perhaps a dagger here and there. The Romans fought back in little groups as best they could, and again the battle hinged (according to Caesar) on his handling of the galleys, which he used to bring reserves to the point where they were needed most. The counter-attack slackened, and the Romans slowly waded ashore, refinding their courage and cohesion with the feel of land. The opposition swiftly dissolved as the armoured array moved in mass across the beach. The first organised invaders (so it would appear) had arrived on British soil.

Having wearily made their bridgehead defensible, the Romans were cheered by the peaceful offerings made to them over the next few days, including Commius, released from his chains, and a number of hostages. Caesar's one remaining aim was to learn more about the land he had invaded, and he could not do this without his cavalry. On the fourth day their ships were sighted, but now a storm arose and drove them back. When combined with the high tide that came with the full moon that night, taking the Romans by surprise, this storm inflicted great damage on Caesar's warships and transports, filling him with fear of being stranded. The flow of hostages and friendly gestures abruptly ended.

Foraging and repair work therefore became the two urgent tasks, and the two legions achieved considerable success at both. However, Legio VII were badly taken by surprise while gathering grain with arms grounded, which shows that they cannot have been much impressed by the offensive capacity displayed by the Britons on the beach. Suddenly the Britons were in among them on their ponies and in their rough little chariots, yelling their war cries and hurling their javelins, in some cases by men balanced on the shaft between the two ponies pulling a chariot. An observant sentry on the bridgehead earthworks – probably on the slight ridge of Sholden Down just west of Deal (3552) – reported a dust cloud rising, and Caesar at once set off with all the troops he could muster. He found Legio VII crowded together, assailed by missiles from all sides. The Britons drew back on Caesar's approach, and after a brief confrontation Caesar withdrew his troops to camp. Only a few had been killed but all had had a great fright.

The Britons were emboldened to launch an attack on the Roman camp. However, it was not unexpected and was decisively repulsed, and thanks to some horsemen brought over by Commius, Caesar was able to strike back at the moment of the Britons' retreat. This gained him further hostages and a most timely respite, for he was in a great hurry to return to Gaul before the gales of equinox. Since all but twelve of his ships had by now been repaired, he was able to do this on that very night, taking his hostages with him. Next morning the Britons found their shore clear of the enemy and could eagerly examine the first Roman remains. It was the end of an eighteen-day wonder.

Although it was an undignified departure for a great conqueror, the Roman Senate granted a thanksgiving lasting a record twenty days, thus paying an unconscious tribute to the primitive Britons and their hostages on display. Caesar was determined to return for a longer stay, and for this purpose he assembled five legions (out of eight under his command in Gaul), 2,000 cavalry, and a large supporting force of auxiliaries. Many smaller boats were specially built to facilitate landing, bringing his fleet to a strength of no less than 800 transports and twenty-eight warships. The problems of assembling this huge armada were aggravated by disturbances in Gaul, and again it sailed later than intended, at nightfall on July 6, 54 BC.

This time the tide carried the boats round the South Foreland, and when day broke they had a distant view of land on the port side. They appear to have been adjacent to the mouth of the Wantsum Channel, which divided the Isle of Thanet from the mainland, and had only to turn westwards to land on the beach chosen by Caesar, as a result of reconnaissance during his previous visit. This was two or three miles north of his original landing place, probably where Sandwich is today or slightly southwards of it, this then being the line of the coast. To reach it, which they did by midday, the troops had to row, and they received high praise from Caesar for their great exertion.

The landing was quite unopposed. As Caesar learned from an informer, the Britons had taken fright at the size of the armada and had fled inland to concentrate on the defence of their defended town, to reach which he had to rely entirely on guidance by prisoners. Knowing nothing of the land, except for what his informers told him, he resolved on a blow of great audacity, a night march followed by a dawn attack, and he duly set off after dark, leaving only ten cohorts and 300 horse as guard for his ships at anchor. The greater part of this awesome march into the interior must have been along the track running westwards from Richborough (of which harbour Caesar apparently had no knowledge) initially along the line of what is now the Canterbury-Sandwich road and later swinging southward past the site of Bekesbourne (1955). They reached the River Great Stour, which was then at estuary width as far as Fordwich (1859), some time after daybreak, and this must have been a march of rather more than the 12 miles estimated by Caesar.

There is no dispute today that the fortified camp of the Britons was Bigbury (1157) and an excellent view of it can be obtained from the point where Caesar must have hit the river, the ford at 126569, which is approached from the east along Tonford Lane, off the main road. The objective will be seen to consist of a pair of flat-topped hills of a combined width of some 1,000 yards, with trees on the top and orchards on the forward slope. Excavations have revealed a triple defence ditch, and signs of artificial steepening can be observed from the lanes that run around and across it.

A greater part of the forward slope was covered by woodland in Caesar's day, and no sooner had the leading Roman cavalry crossed the ford than they were charged by horsemen and chariots. They drove them back, and now the Romans found their way forward blocked by a deep ditch and by logs across all entrances into the wood. After further attacks had been driven back, Legio VII advanced to the ditch with shields interlocked, forming tortoise, and under cover of this a causeway was made across the ditch, presumably by the laborious process of pushing earth and faggots between the legs of the shield bearers. The javelins and bolts hurled by the Britons cannot have achieved any penetration, and this must have greatly depressed them, for they put up little fight once the tortoise had completed its creeping passage of the ditch. The Romans took occupation of this great fortified settlement and consolidated for the night.

Next day, Caesar had already sent mixed cavalry and infantry groups off in pursuit of the enemy when news arrived that his ships at anchor had been shattered by a storm. He recalled his pursuit force and brought the entire army back to the coast, since every man was needed to repair the damage and to haul the 760 surviving boats up the beach out of reach of wave; it was a heavy price to pay for his failure to locate the sheltered waters around Richborough. This allowed the Britons ten days' respite and they put them to the remarkably progressive use of forming a single command under a chieftain from north of the Thames, Cassivellaunus.

When Caesar resumed his invasion it soon emerged that the Britons had decided to rely entirely on hit-and-run tactics and to avoid a pitched battle, at any rate south of the Thames. The first clash may have occurred on the Downs south of the Stour, and although the Roman cavalry easily drove off their attackers, they ran into a trap and suffered loss in the exuberance of pursuit. Having reoccupied Bigbury, or some further camp, the Romans were amazed to see their outpost screen bisected by raiders as they worked on their positions. Two large cohorts were quickly deployed in support, but the raiders cut through the narrow gap between them and galloped off the field. This gave the Romans great anxiety. But next day the Britons overplayed their hand, and having fallen on the closely escorted foraging parties of three legions they were smitten by a swift counter-attack and could not evade punishing pursuit by a large cavalry force.

This gave Caesar access to the Thames without further opposition. He found that there was one ford across it – which may have been below Westminster, for whereas the Stour has subsided the Thames has swollen – and that the far bank bristled with spikes and had a large force of defenders. Caesar at once 'sent the cavalry in advance', presumably by swimming at some other point, and his legions crossed by the ford almost simultaneously, with only their heads above water. The defenders' morale broke under these shock tactics, and they fell back on a large but well concealed defended town, or oppidum, which was probably Wheathampstead, Hertfordshire.

After great difficulty, Caesar succeeded in locating this stronghold among the woods, with aid from local enemies of Cassivellaunus. He duly took it by storm, although without capturing Cassivellaunus. Meanwhile the chieftains in Kent had shown their loyalty to the combined cause by making an assault on the Roman bridgehead by Sandwich. It was decisively repulsed, the ten cohorts (from different legions) admirably justifying their selection for this task.

Now disturbing news from Gaul reached Caesar. He made terms with Cassivellaunus and ordered his legions back to the coast. They brought so many prisoners and hostages with them that it was intended that the ships should make two hauls. However, contrary winds impeded this plan, and most ships made only the one crossing, heavily laden. Thus this second invasion came to its end in mid-September, having lasted a little more than two months.

By the terms he enforced on the British tribes Caesar was able to exercise a form of suzerainty over them from Gaul. This was to endure, and Christ was to be born and crucified before Roman troops were again seen in Britain. However, Caesar's ally Commius made a swift return with his Atrebatic warriors. They gained the Isle of Wight in 50 BC and expanded along the mainland coast as far as the Selsey or Manhood Peninsula (SZ 8592). A continuous ditch, 10 miles long, was dug for the defence of their Sussex bridgehead, and parts of it can still be seen, as indicated on the 1:50,000 map (SU 8206, 8406, 8607) just to the north of Chichester. Already impinging on the domain of the Trundle, the bridgehead of the Atrebates was to expand further, which meant that Sussex also came under Roman influence.

Over the Medway

Chapter 3

THE ROMAN CONQUEST

Sheer ambition was the primary motive that impelled Roman emperors towards the conquest of Britain. The first to try, Gaius (or Caligula) in 39 AD, was thwarted by a mutiny in his intended assault force, showing that fear of the Ocean still exerted a powerful hold, especially in the absence of inspired leadership. Claudius, who followed, at least had the excuse that two brothers, Caractacus and Togodumnus, who had jointly inherited a kingdom north and south of the Thames, showed contempt of their treaty obligations to Rome and were bent on expanding their kingdom. Claudius planned to purge them of their contempt by a full-scale invasion. He entrusted it to Aulus Plautius, who assembled four legions, but once again mutiny broke out at the prospect of crossing the Ocean. However, a talk by one of Claudius's ministers, the former slave (and therefore derided) Narcissus, shamed the soldiers into obedience.

This third Roman expedition lacks a chronicler of Caesar's authority, and many important details are unknown. It set out, probably in April 43, in three divisions directed to different harbours, but it appears that only the most easterly reached its destination, Richborough (TR 3260), and that the others eventually joined it there. It is certain that the Romans did now make use of the harbour of Richborough, to which accumulations of shingle down the spit from Thanet had probably begun to make access devious.

The two king-brothers do not appear to have been expecting the Romans, for the landing was unopposed. However, they soon appeared separately on the scene and were separately routed in two skirmishes somewhere in East Kent. Plautius advanced on Canterbury, where the Belgae had formed a settlement, and established a fortified camp nearby, possibly at Harbledown (1357), on the promontory now containing a housing estate.

Plautius continued the advance to Rochester, where the Belgae had also founded a settlement, and found the enemy waiting in strength beyond the Medway, which had yet to be widened (with the Thames) by a shift in the sea bed. He had some Gallic mercenaries who were specially trained to swim in full equipment, and they swam the river, probably in the vicinity of the M2 bridge. They were attacked by horsemen and chariots and retaliated by the agile tactic of slashing the ponies' legs, which would not have been so easy if the chariots had been fitted with swords on their wheel-hubs. Legio II then made a crossing, it would appear by a ford further upstream. Although initially surprised, the Britons made a desperate attempt to drive them back, and night fell with both sides locked in hectic combat. The Romans succeeded in feeding another legion into their bridgehead, and after its commander had been almost captured in the fighting next morning, they at last put the enemy to flight. It was extremely rare for a battle to last so long, and maybe both sides fought with the awareness that it would decide the fate of Britain, as indeed proved to be the case.

When the Romans reached the Thames the mercenaries again proved their prowess at swimming, while other troops found or built a bridge further upriver. There was some fierce skirmishing in the forest beyond the river. Both sides had their losses, and on the British they included King Togodumnus, who was killed.

The scene was now set for the entry of Emperor Claudius, and in due course (maybe August) he appeared, bringing with him some of the Praetorian Guard and some elephants, who came for the prestige they could inspire rather than for utility. Claudius crossed the Thames as if leading an assault and made triumphant progress to the British capital, Camulodunum, or Colchester, and there received the surrender of many tribes eager to join the winning side. He left Britain in September, having instructed Plautius to complete the conquest of the island.

The only part where this presented no problem was the kingdom of Cogidumnus, covering most of Sussex. Indeed, he had continued the tradition of alliance with Rome and had thoroughly approved of the action against Caractacus. He alone was allowed to retain the title of king under Roman rule. Nevertheless, it appears that the march of the Romans met resistance at Mount Caburn (TQ 4408), for Roman scabbards and other trappings have been found there, next to the charred remains of the wooden gateway.

Elsewhere it was less easy, and the North and Welsh West were never to be subdued. Not until 51 was Caractacus captured, near the Welsh border, to become the eleventh British king whose surrender is recorded on Claudius's triumphal arch and to gain his liberty by a moving appeal to him in Rome. In 60 or 61 the East Anglican Iceni tribe rose in revolt, led by their late king's widow, Boadicea, who had herself come literally under the Romans' lash. Having sacked Colchester, they marched on the great Roman creation, London. General Suetonius, who had succeeded Plautius, was busy subduing homicidal Druids in Anglesey. He personally reached London ahead of Boadicea but saw that there was no hope of concentrating enough troops for the defence of the town, which was thus left to the wrath of the Iceni. They made a throrough job of its sacking, slaughtering everyone regardless of origin and burning every building. They then moved northwards, applied the same treatment to St Albans, and confronted the two legions brought from Anglesey by Suetonius. Although vastly outnumbered, the Romans gained the victory and killed all their opponents, male and female, in a fight to the death. It was probably the heaviest day's slaughter ever suffered by the British race.

The Londoners had paid a terrible price for collaborating with the Romans, and it is remarkable that the town should have been rebuilt on the same site. No doubt the whole of the South-East trembled, but the extermination of the Iceni discouraged attempts at emulation, and collaboration could soon be peacefully and profitably continued. The South-East formed a most important link in the Romans' lines of communication for their frontier war in the North and West. As will be described in greater detail in the next chapter, the harbours of Kent were linked by straight roads to Canterbury, and thence to London, whence the reinforcements could continue in a north-westerly direction up Watling Street, head due north up Ermine Street, or march north-east to Colchester. This area of passage must have been abuzz with stories of the fighting, told by returning soldiers in many strange tongues, and there must also have been many colourful merchants from overseas, drawn by the prosperity Roman soldiers and administrators brought with them. The people of the South-East are unlikely to have observed the scene with anything more than passing interest, having no sense of unity as Britons. And so it continued until the year 212 or 214, when they were given new identification with the occupying power, for in this year the Emperor Caracalla issued an edict conferring Roman citizenship on all free subjects of the Empire.

Rutupiae

Chapter 4

THE SHORE FORTS

It is believed that raiders from the German coast first disturbed the orderly calm of the Roman occupation as early as 200 AD or thereabouts. However, they did not present a serious menace until some seventy years later, and only now did the Romans take steps to turn their lines of communication into a fully fortified zone. The coastal fortresses were built at different times. The remains of four can be found in Kent and one in Sussex, together with three in East Anglia and one in Hampshire.

The most northerly and oldest of the four in Kent stood on the tongue of land that jutted into the Wantsum Channel from the mainland at its northern mouth. This was a feature of great importance, named Regulbium and later Reculver (TR 2269 – DoE), and if approached along the lane from the Roman Galley Hotel (2267) it is easy enough to envisage the water filling the low ground on the southern side of the promontory and providing good shelter for ships. Unfortunately the only prominent monuments left are the splendid towers of a Saxon church founded in 669, which today rise contemptuously over a garish mass of caravans. This was built in the middle of a square formed by wall and defence ditch, measuring just under 200 yards each side. Some remains of the wall, and of the east and south gates, are visible.

At the southern end of the Wantsum Channel, protected by a sandbank round which the Stour flows into the sea, was the long established harbour of Rutupiae or Richborough (3260 – DoE), at the side of an island-mound connected to the mainland by causeway. This stood at the end of the Ancient Way and is thought to have formed the Britons' main link with Europe. The Romans developed it as a sophisticated base town, and to celebrate Claudius's conquest of Britain, as a symbol to be seen far out at sea, they built a huge monument with marble pillars, of which the base can still be seen. It had its own wall and defence ditches, and in the latter half of the 3rd Century fortress walls were built around the whole complex, of much the same measurements of those at Reculver, forming a rectangle almost 200 yards long on north and south sides and slightly less on east and west. Enough remains of the fort to provide a marvellous memorial to Roman industry, for on the west side the walls still display their might, almost to their original dimensions of a width of 12 feet and a height of 30, and the double ditches, of both an outer and inner perimeter, must be almost as deep as originally dug. Remains also exist of the ditch built when the Romans began their occupation in 43. There is no better example left of the power and majesty of Roman fortification, and it is appropriate that it should adorn what was their main port of entry, their gateway into Britain.

At Dover (Dubris) the only relic still readily visible is the lighthouse (or pharos) on Castle Hill, which although reduced in size and overshadowed by the Saxon church next to it remains a great beacon of Roman achievement. The supreme importance of Dover dawned on the Romans in the second half of the 2nd Century, when they built a fort on the west side of the lagoon into which the now diminished River Dour flowed and which in those days lay well to the east of the present harbour basin. Recent excavations have established the line of this fort, which for a time was the chief base of the Roman fleet, and also the line of a larger overlapping fort on its north-east side. (See map on page 22.) Both Castle Hill and the Western Heights were fortified, and a pharos was also built on the latter; it was named the Bredenstone and remained as a monument until demolished in the cause of defence against Napoleon. Thus twin porchlights beckoned the Romans' ships into the harbour that seemed designed by nature to form the main gateway between Britain and Europe.

Twelve miles west of Dover stood the fort known as Stutfall Castle (1134), guarding the port of Lympne (Lemanis), which lay on the estuary of the River Limen. Although shifts of the hillside long ago turned it into forlorn heaps of stone, which lie on private ground, the outline of its wall and ramparts is easily distinguishable from the lane flanking it on the south side of the Royal Military Canal. Second in size to Reculver, it extended 350 yards from the waterfront, enclosing 10½ acres, which would comfortably have accommodated 1,000 men. The Limen entered the sea roughly where Hythe is and was flanked on the south side by mudflats and the sand or shingle bank of the present coastline. There can have been little hope of a successful raid on the galleys lying at anchor or mooring, for not only was the fort itself in a dominating position but excellent observation could be obtained from the steep banks overlooking it from east and west. Yet the fact of the fortifications shows that the Saxon raiders were people to be feared.

Although the main object of the forts was to safeguard ships of war, providing security for their crews, cover for the garrison, and a base for swift counter-attack, it is certain that Lympne filled a function as a base port second in importance only to Richborough, and whereas the tracks to Richborough and Dover had only to be improved, a new road had to be built inland from Lympne, the fine, straight, and evocative Stone Street. All converged on Canterbury (Durovernum), which itself had to be fortified. There is evidence that earthworks were thrown up round this important centre at an early age, and a wall, enclosing 130 acres, was very probably built before any of the shore forts, for it had inward turrets, a style known to have been abandoned between 270 and 285. This wall formed the foundation of the medieval wall, and many of its remains, including some massive entrance gates, have recently been traced, thanks partly to German bombing.

A few soldiers were probably kept at Canterbury for protective duties, but it was certainly not a major garrison town. The nearest military station may have been at Ospringe, around the chapel that can be seen in part at TQ 994613, which would have meant a march of some 24 miles from the base ports. The next fortified camp on the route to London was at Joyden's Wood, 30 miles beyond Ospringe, via the bridge at Rochester (Durobrivae), which town also had a formidable defence wall, although covering a smaller area than Canterbury's. Joyden's Wood (near Dartford) is 18 miles from London, and (unless taken by sea) reinforcements for the Northern front must have marched right through the city, having only one bridge to cross, and observed the great defence wall, which enclosed 330 acres, running on the east side past the site of the Tower.

In Sussex, the Romans made use of the harbour at Hastings, but did not build a fort, although they regarded the place of sufficient importance to carve a path through the Andredsweald and build a road that joined the main one at Rochester. The best shelter for warships was further westwards, inside the inlet of sea covering what is now the Pevensey Levels. On a tongue of land jutting into it from the west, the magnificent fort of Anderida Castle (TQ 646048 – DoE) was built. Apart from Portchester, in Hampshire, this is the only sea fort to have survived (almost) intact, and it is given added fascination by its less durable Norman additions and its Churchillian ones. Oval in shape, with a maximum length of 300 yards, it displays ten solid turrets, jutting outwards and thus dating themselves as late 3rd Century at the earliest. Since the Andredsweald throttled access inland, this can be classified as a purely naval fort, acting as shield on the seaward side of the harbour.

Further westwards, 50 miles away, there was an important base port at Fishbourne (SU 8304), supplying the Western front. Lying at the end of a long estuary, this was not given elaborate fortification, although a commander of great status appears to have lived nearby, judging from the splendid palace that has been unearthed. Only two miles to the east lay the town believed to have been founded by Cogidumnus and given the name of Noviomagus before that of Chichester. This had a fine wall around it, a portion of which still stands serene with two outward turrets on the south-west side and is in full view from the ring road.

It appears that at least two of the sea forts, those at Richborough and Lympne, were built as defence, not against Saxons, but against Romans. Their builder, a Belgic named Carausius, held command of the Roman fleet, the Classis Britannica, which operated in boats propelled by oar from either side of the Channel, with headquarters at Boulogne. Because of the deals he made with raiders, Carausius was in 286 summoned to Rome by the Emperor Diocletian, but he defied the order and declared himself Emperor of Britain, thus becoming the country's first independent ruler. As was apt to happen to such men, he was murdered six years later, whereupon his killer, Allectus, was confronted by a large invasion force sent by Diocletian, who had at last mustered the requisite naval force. Contrary to the expectations of Allectus, a landing was made as far west as Hampshire, and having switched his troops from Kent, he met death and defeat in a battle near the site of Basingstoke. Trembling with fear of being plundered by defeated mercenaries, the Londoners were saved by the timely arrival of the Roman commander, Constantius, come straight from Boulogne. He was accorded a hero's welcome, after which Britain placidly reverted to the rule of Rome and again waxed prosperous.

The Classis Britannica was not reformed as such and its place was in part taken by a new command, bearing the resonant title of Count (Comes) of the Saxon Shore. All nine of the sea forts came under him – three in East Anglia, four in Kent, one in Sussex, and the ninth at Portchester, just west of Portsmouth – and no doubt they made their contribution to the seventy years of peace that followed. It was broken with great pain and violence in 367, when Picts and Scots swarmed over the northern wall, and Saxons and Franks fell upon the coast. The Duke of Britain and the Count of the Saxon Shore were both killed, and their troops deserted in large numbers, turning themselves into marauding bands and spreading fear and chaos. However, the Emperor Valentinian could call on a resolute and efficient man in Theodosius. Landing at Richborough with four regiments, he marched on London and rapidly restored order, partly by firmness, partly by an amnesty to deserters. He then set about reorganising the defences.

A location list – the Notitia Dignitatum – drawn up near the end of the 4th Century shows that troops were brought in from far away to garrison the Saxon Shore forts, even at risk of weakening the frontier defences. There was a unit of Tungrians at Dover, of Turnacensians at Lympne, and a cohort of Vetasians at Reculver, all mercenary troops from across the Channel, and Richborough housed the headquarters of Legio II, which had been transferred from Caerleon in Wales, while foreign troops of unknown origin, Abulci, garrisoned Anderida. It was a pity that the British people had to rely on these strange foreigners, rather than organise their own local defence. They were soon to regret it.

Chapter 5

JUTES, SAXONS, DANES

Roman Britain was denuded of troops by the rebellious adventures of her rulers. Among the first was Magnus Maximus. He led an expedition to Gaul and was there killed and defeated in 388. Another was a Briton who took the illustrious name of Constantine and was elected Emperor by his own mutinous troops after two similarly elected had in turn been murdered. He drained Britain of troops in order to fight Vandals and other tribes in Gaul, and after a series of victories stretching as far afield as Spain, he was lured to Rome, to defeat and execution.

Spread between 407 and 411, the adventures of Constantine brought about the final collapse of Roman rule in Britain, as was acknowledged by the Emperor Honorius in 410 by his reply to a plea for military aid: 'The cantons should take steps to defend themselves.' This was a thing that the Britons were in no state to do, and for the next six hundred years they were constantly being trampled upon by invaders, who, being unable to write, allowed the era to acquire the sombre name of Dark Ages. The military history is a blur, penetrated by only a few flickers of light cast by monastic chroniclers writing long after the event without any certainty of accuracy.

The first invaders to make their mark were two brothers bearing the memorable names of Hengist and Horsa. They are said to have been Jutes, whose origin baffles historians, and to have come as replacements for the departed mercenaries at the invitation of the ruler of Britain, Vortigern. Apparently they were offered the Isle of Thanet as reward, and tradition has it that they landed on the promontory of Ebbsfleet, on the island's south-east tip, probably in an earlier year than that stated in the Anglo-Saxon Chronicle, 449.

These legendary warriors drove away raiding Picts and sent for reinforcements, telling the people back home 'of the worthlessness of the Britons and of the excellence of the land' (again to quote the Chronicle). A positive migration of Jutes, Saxons, and Angles followed, and Vortigern, not surprisingly, found himself attacked by the warriors he had invited. In a battle at Aylesford (TQ 7258) – a place of High Belgic and Roman culture – Horsa was slain but Vortigern was driven back over the Medway, which became the early boundary of Kent, dividing the Men of Kent from their subsequent compatriots on the west bank, the Kentish Men. Hengist advanced beyond the Medway in military partnership with his reported son, Aesc, and inflicted a shattering defeat on the Britons at Crayford (5175). It is recorded that 4,000 of them were slain and that 'the Britons then forsook Kent and fled to London in great terror'.

Hengist and Aesc appear to have been uninterested in London, which seems odd. They spent the next twenty years in enslaving such natives as could still be found in Kent, and then turned upon some warlike Britons in Sussex or Surrey. Two battles are mentioned in the Chronicle, and the result of the second, attributed to 473, was that 'the Welsh fled from the English like fire'. This is a revealing entry, showing that the chronicler regarded the non-Anglo-Saxon inhabitants of Roman Britain as foreigners, for which the word Welsh was considered an adequate substitute, and that Hengist and his heirs and allies, instead of being invaders, were thought to have become worthy representatives of the home side, the English. It would seem to be the earliest usage of the word.

Hearing rather belatedly of the plunder to be reaped, a Saxon warrior named Aelle set out with his sons Cymen, Wlencing, and Cissa in a year reported as 477. They landed on the coast of what they were to make the kingdom of the South Saxons, Sussex. Having established a bridgehead astride Selsey Bill, which extended further into the sea than today, they routed the local warriors, driving them into the Andredsweald, and took possession of Noviomagus, which was renamed Chichester because Cissa set up his camp there. From its inconclusive reporting in the Chronicle, it seems that the Saxons may well have been worsted in a battle fought in 485 at a place bafflingly named Mearc Raedsburn, which might be Slonk Hill (TQ 2205), north of Shoreham, where the legend of a famous victory still survives. Anyway, not until 490 – thirteen years since their coming – did the Saxons lay siege to the Britons' last stronghold, Anderida Castle, Pevensey. Aelle and Cissa were together in charge, and having at last stormed the great Roman walls, they killed all its occupants; 'there was not even one Briton left.' Ill-prepared for war though they undoubtedly were, the Britons must at least have fought hard enough to arouse the wrath of Aelle and Cissa.

Aelle superseded Hengist as the leading warrior of his day and was acknowledged as Bretwalda, or overlord, of all England south of the Humber. He too does not appear to have coveted London, which fell to the East Saxons, founders of Essex. Although the history of London at this time is even more obscure than others, it appears that a breakaway group formed their own kingdom there before the 9th Century, becoming known as the Middle Saxons, founders of Middlesex.

In the west and north of Roman Britain there was a stronger military tradition, and indeed it produced a great chieftain in Arthur, who halted the advance of the Saxons. Subsequently Hengist's descendant Ethelbert, who was King of Kent from 560 to 616, had his moment of supremacy, for he too was acknowledged as Bretwalda, although the only record of his military activities is of defeat by Ceawlin of Wessex. Ethelbert of course gained greater fame by being the first king in England to embrace Christianity. It was eighty years before it spread to Sussex, which shows that the Andredsweald was still throttling communication between the two kingdoms. Both had by now settled to a remarkably cosy and cultured life under the descendants of the fiery warriors who had established their kingdoms there.

It was left to the other kingdoms to vie for supremacy. For a time it was held by the Northumbrians, who had by 617 subdued the whole of England except Kent. Then it was the turn of the West Saxons, whose restless Prince Cadwalla slew King Ethelwalch of Sussex in a battle placed by tradition on the down south-east of Stoughton (SU 8010) in about 683. Cadwalla was driven out by two of the dead king's ealdormen but returned in 686, now King of Wessex, and invaded both Sussex and Kent. In 687 the Kents turned on the invaders and burned Cadwalla's brother Mul to death with twelve of his followers. But in 694 they were brought to heel by Ine, Cadwalla's successor as King of Wessex, and forced to pay huge tribute.

Subsequently the Mercians gained such ascendancy that their King Offa could claim to be (the first) King of the English. Kent disputed his authority and, after three years of defiance, did battle against him at Otford (TQ 5259) in 774. The vagueness of the entry in the Chronicle indicates at the very least a check for Offa, and indeed not until 805 did Kent become a province of Mercia. Twenty years later King Egbert of Wessex gained dominance by military means and put an end to the rule of the southern kings, even as vassals, after some obscurely reported fighting. Northwards of the Thames he established himself as overlord, making England almost one nation.

Now came the Danes or Vikings – men from any of the countries of Scandinavia – and inflicted great and savage loss on the English. Kent was an obvious target for these cruel raiders in their long-boats, for Canterbury was acknowledged as the religious head of England at a time when religion both greatly influenced politics and attracted great material wealth as spiritual offering, and Rochester was also a religious centre of importance, having its own bishop. Both were conveniently close to the coast, and in the great obsession with culture it would appear that the inhabitants of neither had done much to maintain the walls and ramparts built around them with Roman expertise some five hundred years earlier. Nor did they maintain the shore forts, neither the ships that operated from them, the troops that garrisoned them, nor the defence walls around them.

The first indication of the Danes' coming to Kent is the entry in the Chronicle for 832: 'The heathen devastated Sheppey.' (i.e. the island adjoining the north coast – but scholars insist that the date should be 835.) Six years later they are reported to have slain many people on the Romney Marsh and to have caused 'great slaughter' in London and Rochester, presumably inside their walls. During the winter of 850-851 they were in permanent occupation of Thanet, and this was immediately followed by the arrival of 350 ships in the mouth of the Thames, from which bands of intrepid men – around fifty from each boat, armed only with long swords, spears, and axes – swooped upon London and Canterbury, having captured ponies to speed their progress, stormed and sacked these cities, and routed an army of Mercian levies in open battle. However, the Saxons struck back. King Ethelwulf (who had succeeded his father Egbert) won a victory at a place reported as Acleah, in which he 'made the greatest slaughter of the heathen host that we have ever heard tell of'; although probably in Surrey it is claimed by some to have been at Oakleigh, 5 miles east of Gravesend. Then Athelstan, another son of Egbert who had been given Kent and Sussex as a sub-kingdom of Wessex, 'destroyed a great host at Sandwich' in a naval battle from which he emerged with nine enemy ships in his possession. It is to be supposed that the Saxons used grappling tactics, and they may have caught the Vikings at tidal disadvantage against the cliffs of Thanet. This is the first evidence that Sandwich had taken over the function of Richborough, probably because of the enlargement of the spit from Thanet.

These two victories brought only temporary respite, for the Vikings returned in 855 and during the next ten years wrought constant torment from bases either on Sheppey or Thanet. But in 865 they turned their attention to East Anglia, where there was no West Saxon army to bar their path, and launched a large and lasting invasion, which in due course gained them control of most of England, including London. Kent and Sussex, remarkably, were about the only parts free from scourge by the Danes at this time. Then came King Alfred's great victory at Edington in 878, and the Danes withdrew into East Anglia. In 885 they reappeared in Kent, coming up the Medway and laying siege to Rochester. This brought about Alfred's entry into Kent, and he forced the Danes back to their boats while the citizens still held their defence walls. Alfred now went to the relief of London, which had certainly suffered severe financial exactions from the Danes if nothing worse. He made his entry, at the cost only of some vindictive killings by the departing Danes, and handed the city over to Ethelred of Mercia, who organised a proper system of defence, including a strengthening of the walls and the levying of a home guard, named the burhware.

In 892 the Danes again launched a great invasion, and this time Kent was their first and primary objective, to be severed by a double-pronged assault through the north and south shores. The southern prong consisted of an armada from Boulogne of 250 long-boats that made entry up the River Rother, which had replaced the silted Limen as a main waterway and had Old Romney (TR 0325) near its mouth. (See map on p 12.) Four miles upriver the Danes came to the edge of the Andredsweald and were confronted with one of the forts, or burhs, which had belatedly been built on instructions from Alfred. This one, which may have been at Stone Cliff (TQ 9426), was only half built and manned by a few coerls or workmen. It quickly fell, and the Danes continued upriver to Appledore, where they built a fortified camp, of which the unusual shape of spur at 955291 may be a solitary relic.

The northerly prong consisted of eighty ships under the redoubtable veteran Hasten, who had recently launched a great attack on Paris. He came up the Swale and established a bridgehead at Milton Regis (8964), thus cutting the Canterbury-Rochester road. His boats would have been moored in Milton Creek, and the mounds on either side of it might have been thrown up by the 4,000 men they brought.

The two prongs made no haste to link up, being content to secure their bases and exert strangulating pressure by plundering all food and booty that lay within their overlapping reach. Alfred's opening ploy was to parley with Hasten, to impress on him the wonders of the Christian faith, and to bribe him to go away. This gave time for the assembly of the mobile militia, the fyrd, as reinforcement for the trusted thanes and their retainers; half the fyrd were embodied in expectation of eventual relief by the other half, so that their land could be kept tilled. To these were added the local burhware, from whose stockades the troops opened a campaign of offensive patrolling to counter that of the enemy. Alfred positioned his army 'at a point as nearly as possible equidistant from each' of the two Danish armies (to quote the Chronicle) which would put it on Charing Heath (9349) on the outskirts of the great forest. From here fighting patrols sought out roaming bands of Danes 'both by day and by night'.

Hasten accepted Alfred's bribe and duly removed himself, only to turn up again at Benfleet, on the northern mouth of the Thames, where the Danes had been long established. The Appledore expedition now moved to link up with Hasten, some going to Benfleet in their boats, others by march route, using captured ponies. The latter set off westwards to make maximum use of the cover of the Andredsweald. Keeping track of their movements, Alfred's son Edward took a mounted force along the track on the North Downs and fell on the Danes after they had reached Farnham, in Surrey. He completely routed them and drove them across the Thames to bay on an island in the River Colne somewhere north of Uxbridge. Here the Danes gained respite by the departure of the serving half of the fyrd before the other half had arrived to relieve them. This enabled them to complete their journey to Benfleet. Edward reassembled the fyrd and brought his men to London, where he was joined by Ethelred and his Mercians and the London burhware. Together they marched on Benfleet and made a daring attack on the fortified camp just as Hasten was returning with his main army from a plundering expedition. They gained great success, smashing the Danes' boats and returning to London with loads of human and material booty, including the wife and two sons of Hasten. Alfred, typically, returned the wife and sons.

Thus Kent was delivered from a threat of terrifying proportions, and the people of London received the terrific and so far unique boost to their morale of participation in a resounding victory, with its fruits immediately displayed to them. Their burhware were in action again two years later (895) when the Danes sailed up the River Lea, which joined the Thames east of London, and dug themselves in. Having failed to eject them by direct assault, Alfred blocked the river. The Danes thereupon set off for Wessex on foot, leaving their entire fleet as prize for the Londoners.

It was in the West, appropriately for a man of Wessex, that Alfred gained his final victory over the Danes. Surlily returning homewards in defeat, the Danes raided a part in which they had previously shown little interest. To quote the Chronicle, 'they harried inland in Sussex near Chichester and the burhware put them to flight, and slew many hundreds of them, and took some of their ships.' It is also on record that in 904, five years after the death of Alfred, the Danes again appeared at the mouth of the Rother and landed on its southern bank. They were promptly driven away by the men of Lydd, who received a grant of land as token of gratitude from their lord, the Archbishop of Canterbury. A big improvement had been brought about in the people's will and capacity to defend their homes.

Alfred's son and grandson, Edward and Athelstan, completed the defeat of the Danes, with help from levies from Kent and London. An eroding period of peace and great prosperity followed. In 978 the weakling Ethelred began the reign that was to earn him the sobriquet of The Unready, and within two years the Danes returned to English shores, Thanet being among the places they visited. In 991 a fleet of ninety-three ships appeared off Folkestone. After making a harrying raid, they went on to Sandwich and thence to Ipswich, where the Danes landed in strength, gained a victory, and were bribed to desist by a payment of Danegeld arranged through Archbishop Sigeric of Canterbury. They returned at similar strength in 994, landing near Gravesend under Olaf and Sweyn, and attempted to take London by storm. Here they 'suffered greater loss and injury than they ever thought possible' but extracted a further bulky slice of Danegeld in exchange for their withdrawing.

Elsewhere in England no one seemed able to inflict loss on the Danes, and when they came up the Medway in 999 and landed near Rochester the performance of the Kentish levies drove the chronicler to the lament: 'Alas! they too quickly yielded and fled, for they had not the support which they should have had.' The result was that the Danes ravaged the whole of West Kent – with or without reducing Rochester is not made clear – and Ethelred attempted a counter-attack by both land and sea. This failed miserably, after exasperating delays in assembly, and indeed 'effected nothing, except the people's distress and waste of money and the emboldening of their foes'.

In 1002 Ethelred purchased respite for the sum of 24,000 pounds. Shortly afterwards he ordered the massacre of Danish residents in England, including King Sweyn's sister. This sharpened the asperity of the contest, and Sandwich was among many parts of England that experienced pillage by Danes at their most merciless. Ethelred decided to build a great fleet, ordering 310 warships to be built by a large variety of coastal towns. Sandwich was chosen as their place of assembly, and they duly came there in 1009. It is typical of the misfortunes of this era that they should have been dissipated by treachery and by storm, the latter destroying the ships pursuing the traitors, and rather than face the Danes in battle the remainder retired to England's one secure harbour, London. This let the Danes into Sandwich once more.

Canterbury's turn came in 1011, having escaped assault two years previously by the payment of 3,000 pounds. This time the Danes were not to be diverted from this city whose name bespoke its importance as the chief burh of Kent. It is probable that the Roman wall had been reinforced by a stockade, and the Danes dug themselves in all round it, throttling every exit. For twenty days the citizens resisted, hurling the Danes back off the walls (if one can believe the lurid account written long after the event by Roger of Hoveden). Then the Danes gained an entry through the treachery of an archdeacon. Horrific stories were told of their doings, of how they set fire to the city, put the defenders to the sword, dragged matrons along by their hair and tossed them into the flames, and of how 'infants, torn from their mothers' breasts, were caught on the points of spears or crushed in pieces under the wheels of wagons'. Archbishop Alphege emerged from the Cathedral in an attempt to stop the killings but was at once hurled back among the monks barricaded inside it, whence to emerge again in surrender when the Danes set fire to the Cathedral roof, thus melting its lead, which cascaded red-hot upon the unfortunate monks. All but four of them were slaughtered.

It was as good a sacking as any of which a Dane could boast, and as a trophy of their doings they carried off Archbishop Alphege. At Greenwich, about a year later, he was offered his life and liberty for 3,000 pounds. He declined to pay and was mockingly put to death, a process mercifully speeded by a Dane whom he had converted to Christianity. The brigands then obtained 48,000 pounds as the price of their departure.

The people of London were again the only Englishmen to gain any glory during the final four years of this terrifying war. In 1013 King Sweyn made a spectacular sweep, which as usual began with a raid on Sandwich and continued northwards by sea. He made a triumphant circuit of England and was seriously opposed only at London, where the burhware were reinforced by King Ethelred himself and his retainers and by the Danish renegade Thorkell the Tall, who had changed sides in disgust at the treatment meted out to St Alphege (as he became). Together they decisively repulsed Sweyn, who lost many men drowned when attempting a crossing of the Thames. However, Ethelred fled to Normandy towards the close of the year, leaving Sweyn master of all England. Only two months later, in February 1014, Sweyn died. Ethelred thereupon returned, and Canute, the youthful son of Sweyn, withdrew his Danes from England, calling at Sandwich after embarking in the north to drop off the hostages he had inherited, having removed their eyes, ears, and hands: a most appropriate memento of his passing.

Canute returned in the summer of 1015. As if to emulate almost every invader since Caesar, he first touched down at Sandwich. He thence took his fleet to the

Dorset coast. Having subdued Wessex, he was opposed by Edmund, a man of far stauncher calibre than his father Ethelred. He was forced back to the defence of London, where in April 1016 Ethelred died and the people declared Edmund king. Edmund set out to restore Wessex to his kingdom, and at this Canute sailed from Dorset to lay siege to London. He took possession of Greenwich and brought his ships as far as Bermondsey, on the south bank of the river. From here his men carved a channel round the southern end of London bridge, thus enabling the long-boats to circumvent it. This skilled and industrious manoeuvre gave the Danes access to the city walls from the west. They threw up earthworks and settled to the siege.

Canute was now diverted westwards but soon returned. Edmund meanwhile was making a march from the West in complete secrecy, which brought him into the huge woods that screened the northern side of London. He turned due southwards at Tottenham, fell upon the Danish siege works from their rear, and sent their occupants rushing to their boats and the south bank of the Thames. Although Edmund's pursuit was delayed by the need to march to Brentford as his nearest crossing place, he brought the Danes to battle on the south bank and defeated them. But his losses were so heavy that he had to return to Wessex to re-form his army.

Canute again resumed the siege. Running low in provisions, he was pushed into making a full-scale assault by land and sea. It was triumphantly repulsed by the Londoners, and Canute withdrew his whole force to the East Anglian coast, where he replenished by plunder. He now took his ships up the Medway and joined up with a force come overland from Essex. But Edmund again made a concealed approach and fell upon the Danes at Otford (where Offa had done battle with Kent in 774). This sent them into precipitate retreat to Sheppey – and it could have been to destruction if they had not retained command of the sea. They reappeared in Essex and brought about a remarkable reversal of the form by inflicting a devastating defeat on Edmund, which began with the flight of some reinforcements from Mercia. Rather than again put Edmund's powers of resilience to the test, Canute came to terms with him and settled for a division of England. This lasted only until November 30 of that year, 1016, when Edmund The Ironside died, and the young Dane was acknowledged King of all England.

Thus England emerged from a long ordeal of invasion, which for the people of Kent in particular probably brought more suffering than any other spate of human oppression. Remarkably few relics of it are to be seen: perhaps a mound or two on either side of the Swale, including what might be a ship burial mound at Harty Ferry (0166); the earthworks on the Roman settlement at Swanscombe (TQ 6172); or at Lesnes Abbey (4778); all were in their bridgehead areas. There is equally little sign of Saxon defences, the only one definitely identified as such being in Sussex, namely the ditch across the spur of Warningcamp Hill (0408), where a burh was established. It is odd that the Saxons built stone churches on such commanding features as Dover Castle Hill and Fort Reculver (TR 2269) but never stone defences. It would be interesting to know whether the churches were intended to form citadels or were put in defended areas for the safety of worshippers — or (more probably) of the treasures inside them. Some believe that most were built for the fortification of man before that of God.

A vivid but haphazard glance into the tensions of life within swoop by Danish raiders may be provided by the holes known as Deneholes that can be found in many parts of Kent. It is haphazard because there can be no guarantee that any particular hole was dug as refuge for either Englishman or Dane, and in any case they are all on private land, liable to be filled in deliberately or by force of nature. Yet many extraordinary shafts have been found, often by accident, drilled to 20 or 30 feet, at a width of perhaps 8 feet, and usually in groups of two or three, at locations ranging from Blackheath to Alkham, near Dover. If nothing else, they add to the mystery of life, and certainly legend may not err in linking the name of Deneholes with the Danish invasion.

Other legends have been perpetuated by gory place names such as Red Lane and Blood Hill. Some may be of fraudulent origin, as for instance their proximity to burial grounds that have been found to have been normal ones. Yet very few of the countless battles fought in the millenium between Caesar and Canute have been located, and of some a legend of bloodshed may be the only genuine relic. Unfortunately legends can have great tenacity without providing clue to origin.

An exhibit of true authenticity is on display at the northern corner of Pegwell Bay (TR 353643). It is a replica of a long-boat, copied from original remains, which was built in Denmark and in 1959 brought to Kent by fifty-three adventurous Danes, of whom there were oars for thirty-two. It provides a fine memorial to the craft of the Viking Danes and can arouse a shudder at the thought of it disgorging its marauders.

Chapter 6

THE NORMAN CONQUEST

From 1016 until 1042 England was under the consecutive rule of three Danes, Canute and his sons Harold and Hardicanute. Made vacant by death, the throne was then restored to a descendant of Alfred and son of Ethelred, Edward, whose piety and mild manner gained him the sobriquet of The Confessor. On his death in January 1066, England had been at peace (of a sort) for fifty years, was much engrossed in culture and religion, and was in great peril, being under the predatory eye of two warlords who both claimed a right to the throne: King Harold Hardrada of Norway, who had established himself as the leading warrior of the day, and Edward's cousin, William Duke of Normandy, who was a descendant of the Danish warrior Rollo. In recognition of the menace the English Witan, or Council, took the unprecedented step of electing a king who had no hereditary claim. His name was Harold.

Harold was the first and only King of England who owed his position to the backing of the people of the South-East. His father was Godwin, an Englishman of obscure origin who married a Dane and gained great influence with Canute, being made Earl of Wessex and ruler of all southern England. He retained his influence under Edward – until he refused to obey his order to 'harry' the people of Dover (by pillage, fire, and sword) as punishment for an offence reported by the Count of Boulogne, that he had been obstructed when trying to obtain lodging there and had lost twenty men killed in a fight with the townsmen, who are also said to have lost twenty killed in this impromptu display of insular defiance. This led to a trial of strength with the King, and to Godwin's flight to

Bruges and Harold's to Ireland. A year later (1052) Godwin landed at Dungeness (which thus gains its first entry into the Chronicle) and won the support of the local seamen there and of those at Hastings. He later joined Harold off the west coast and, sailing eastwards together, they drew naval reinforcements from Pevensey, Romney, Hythe, Folkestone, Dover, and from Sandwich, whence the King's fleet sailed for London just ahead of him. Godwin followed him, plundering Milton Regis and the Isle of Sheppey as he passed through the Swale, and arrived at Southwark with a larger fleet and following than commanded by the King, who had made himself very unpopular through his dealings with Normans during Godwin's absence. Acknowledging the situation, the King welcomed him into the city and fully reinstated him in all his power. Godwin died only a year later, and Harold inherited all the power an Englishman could wield.

Unlike his predecessors of Wessex origin, Harold was consecrated king at Westminster, and this was wholly appropriate, for he recognised, as no other king before him, the great strategic importance of this centre point of the network of roads inherited from the Romans. Certainly he had great need of good communications, for in addition to Harold of Norway and William of Normandy – the latter of whom belligerently claimed that he (Harold) had vowed acknowledgement of William's right to the throne of England – Harold's brother Tostig also presented a threat. He had been driven from his earldom of Northumbria and had been assured the support of King Malcolm of Scotland in any attempt he might make to retrieve it from the usurper whom Harold had recognised as earl. Thus four potential invaders had designs on Harold's England, and there could be no telling where their blows might fall.

In the event Tostig was the first to strike. Having raised an expedition in Flanders, he landed at Sandwich in May 1066 and either by force or defection enlarged his fleet to some sixty ships; despite its long proven attraction to invaders, Sandwich still lacked proper defences. Harold at once set out from London with his household troops, the redoubtable housecarls of Danish origin, and at the same time sent out messengers to summon the thanes, embody the fyrd, and alert his seamen and coastguard levies. This move was to be proved fatally impetuous, for he could not keep his fleet and militiamen permanently mobilised, waiting for the more formidable foes of whose coming Tostig had sounded a false alarm. Tostig put to sea before Harold's arrival. He made a landing up the Humber, was heavily defeated by Edwin and his Mercians, and driven onwards to Scotland with only twelve ships. The defectors from Sandwich deserted him and returned.

Early in September Harold disembodied his militia and withdrew his fleet from the Channel to London, there to undergo repair. A few days later news reached him that another expedition had come up the Humber, containing the combined armies of Tostig and King Harold Hardrada of Norway. Again Harold set off with his housecarls and those of his brothers, Earls Leofwine and Gyrth. He found the invaders ensconced at Stamford Bridge, 8 miles beyond York, having defeated an army of both Mercians and Northumbrians. Harold attacked at once and won a great victory in a ferocious battle, in which both Tostig and the mighty Harold Hardrada were slain.

This battle was on Monday, September 25. On Wednesday the 27th a change of wind gave William of Normandy the chance for which he had been impatiently waiting for over a month. He was of course not to know that the gales that confined his ships to harbour had been blowing greatly to his advantage, by holding him back while the enemy's ships and coastal levies were ready to receive him, and he had had to use all his powers of persuasion to prevent his volatile allies, from Britanny, Flanders, and lesser principalities of France, from dispersing in disgust. But now on this Wednesday evening there was neither foe nor contrary wind to impede the ships that sailed out of the Somme from St Valery. Soon after daybreak next morning they had covered the 65 miles to the Sussex coast. Spirits were high.

Blown further than intended, they had arrived hard by the great cliffs of Beachy Head. The only suitable landing place beyond their shadow to the east was by the old Roman fort of Anderida (TQ 6404), which still lay on a promontory jutting eastwards into the Pevensey shallows. So complete was the demobilisation of the local levies, in their urge to return to the land, that this fort of tremendous potential strength lay empty. The Normans clambered ashore and took occupation, after William had slipped and made first contact with English soil with hands and face: an omen he turned from bad to good by calling out, 'See, I have taken England with both my hands.'

In the matter of chronicling William was no Caesar, and his reported estimate of the size of his expedition as being 3,000 ships and 60,000 troops is without doubt a great exaggeration, perhaps to the extent of tenfold; unfortunately there is no eyewitness account from either side, and a great deal has to be left to conjecture. Certainly it must have been wonderful to see the unfolding of the standards, panoplies, and variegated tentage of the rival barons and knights, to achieve a measure of coordination among whom presented William with his most crucial and exacting test of leadership. Probably at least a third of his troops were mounted, and it cannot have been easy to chivvy their horses – round, sturdy cobs – over the prows of the ships and up the slippery bank of the promontory.

William had brought with him the timber and slave labour to construct a fort and he put it up inside the Roman fort, presumably where the stone castle was later built. But he soon realised that the tiny foothold he had obtained offered no scope whatever for expansion, its exits being throttled by the great Andredsweald, which he found impenetrable on horseback and exhaustingly obstructive on foot. He therefore put to sea again and took occupation of the little port of Hastings, the sailors from which had been withdrawn with the main fleet to London. William placed his collapsible wooden fort on the commanding pinnacle (8209) and sent out parties to plunder and terrify the neighbourhood, while sitting tight in his bridgehead to avoid any severance of his supply line from Normandy: a strategy that had served his Danish ancestors well. His knights

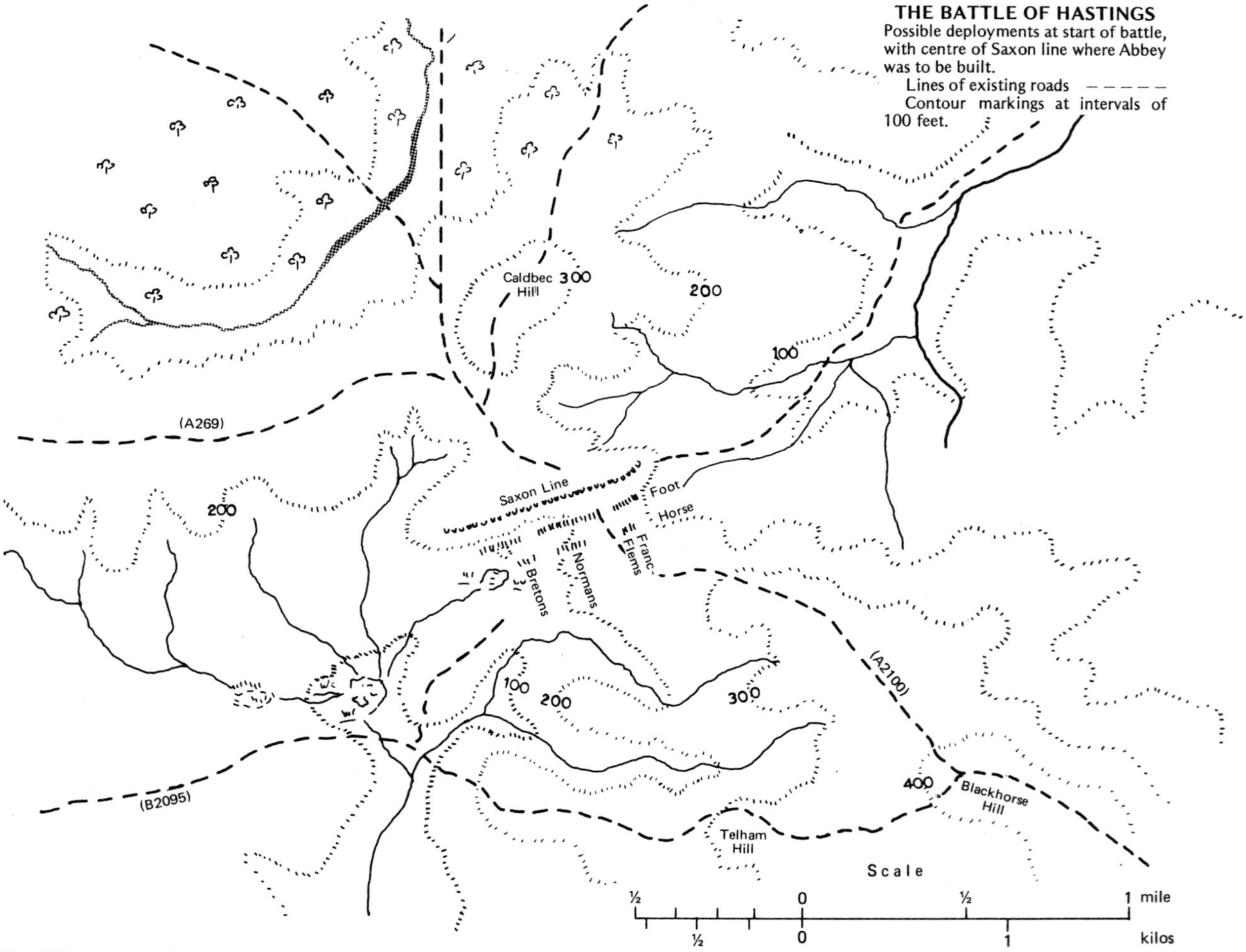

THE BATTLE OF HASTINGS
Possible deployments at start of battle, with centre of Saxon line where Abbey was to be built.
Lines of existing roads — — — — —
Contour markings at intervals of 100 feet.

found scourging the people a pleasant enough duty, except for a seaborne party that either went on reconnaissance or lost their way. They landed at Romney and were there set upon and killed.

By a remarkable feat of communication – presumably by pony and certainly not by beacon – news of William's landing reached Harold at York only three days after its happening, that is on October 1. It took him six days to cover the 196 miles to London, also presumably by pony, accompanied by such of his housecarls as could ride. He waited four days while the summonses went out for the assembly of the fyrd: time enough to bring in only those within some 50 miles. Then on October 11 (so it would appear) he set out for his rendezvous, 'the hoary apple tree', displaying the same impetuosity that had brought death to Hardrada and no doubt waxed all the stronger in consequence. This apple tree stood on what is now Caldbec Hill (7516) and was then part of some heathland by the fringe of the forest, a distance of 64 miles from London, via the Roman road from Rochester. The troops arrived on the evening of October 13. The main fighting element consisted of Harold's housecarls and those of his brothers Leofwine and Gyrth. To these must have been added some levies from London and some brought in by local thanes. Other members of the fyrd were still coming in from east and west, and tradition has it that there was a strong contingent from Kent. Most experts are agreed that it must have been a small force, probably between 6,000 and 7,000, about equal in number to the enemy.

It is unlikely that the English made any attempt to dig in. It was not in their nature to do so, and in any case Harold thought in terms of making a swift surprise attack, not of defence. It therefore came as a shock to him to learn at dawn next morning, Saturday, October 14, that news of his coming had reached William and that he was marching from Hastings to do battle with him. Harold rushed his troops forward to a rather lower ridge connected to Caldbec Hill by a saddle. This is where the town of Battle now stands, and the remains of the Abbey (built by William to expiate Harold's death) mark the centre of Harold's line; it will be noticed that a curve has been made in the Roman road (now designated A2100) to circumvent the Abbey. His right rested on where the ground slopes away beyond the castle-style buildings of the Abbey School, and here the Kent contingent took post. His left must have been on the spur running eastwards from the church, which also provided a slope to protect the flank.

There was much confusion (according to Florence of Worcester) as the troops took position, and much cramming to fit the men into the frontage of about 1,000 yards afforded by the ridge. It was at its worst on the sloping flanks where the fyrd took post, armed as the primitive soldiers they were with a motley of spears, axes, bills, scythes, javelins, hammers, and slings, and clad for the most part in leather jerkins and caps, though some may have had chain-covered shirts and most probably had small shields. The housecarls must have cast disdainful eyes on their peasant comrades. They worked as combat teams, with confidence greatly enhanced by victory, and had their drills for combining the use of their famous double-handled axe with that of the sword, javelin, and small oval shield.

They wore acorn-shaped helmets, jerkins with iron rings attached, trousers of sacking bound by leather thongs, and sandals. They had left their ponies in rear, for having no stirrups they had met disaster trying to fight a mounted action some years previously in Wales. Nor did they have archers, nor catapult artillery; indeed the English had made little advance in weaponry since the days of the Belgae and still relied mainly on dash, though now without the help of horses.

Bent on the type of sudden blow for which Caesar had been famous, William marched out of Hastings soon after sunrise, with a far better balanced and equipped army. Taking the Roman road (A2100) he ascended Blackhorse Hill (7714) and here learned from one of his knights, who had been ahead scouting, that Harold was getting into position on the hill. William's troops must have been spread along all the 3½ miles from Hastings. He ordered them to close up, halt, and don armour. They then advanced in column for a further 1½ miles before deploying for the attack.

Nothing but frustration awaits the visitor who tries to follow the route taken by the Normans along this Roman road, which in those days ran through heathland, broken by the odd gorse bush and the occasional plot of cultivated land. Today the road is flanked by a continual ribbon of houses and gardens, making every likely viewpoint inaccessible. However, the flanking route offers better prospect: turn left just beyond Blackhorse Hill and Inn at signpost marked Crowhurst (770143) and right at road junction 761140 up Telham Hill, from which a good view can be obtained of the Abbey School buildings, representing Harold's army, and of Caldbec Hill with its windmill beyond. About a mile further on this lane joins B2095, and by turning right here the ground over which the attack was made can be examined (on the left) at close quarters and at leisure. Access into the Abbey may be obtained (on payment) from the north side, and here Harold's view of the action may be assessed from the alleged spot at which he fell, but the public are denied the better viewpoint of the school.

The Normans must have swung off the Roman road, in order to deploy, very close to where B2095 joins it. William had formed his force into three divisions, of which the largest consisted of his own Normans. He placed them in the centre, with their right probably on the line of the road. On their right was the Franco-Flemish division, and on the left were the Bretons. As indicated by the pond close to our viewpoint road (746152) the valley below the hill was boggy, and the Bretons must have passed it on their left, with the enemy very close to them on their right, in order to form up for the attack. Having no weapons of longer range than achieved by the might of the arm, the English could only stand and yell defiance as the enemy host went through the ponderous and elaborate procedure of deploying, barely 200 yards from them. This must have been a cold-blooded and spine-chilling performance, most of all for the under-equipped and undertrained fyrd, who must have gaped in awe, if not shock, at this spectacle of the debouching of a modern army, with all its varied and sophisticated paraphernalia. The house-carls would have been less impressed, being sure that William was a lesser foe than the one they had just beaten, Hardrada, and however ragged they may have appeared to the French, the glint of their teeth and of their axes, massed beneath the two standards of Harold, the Dragon of Wessex and the Fighting Man, cannot have sharpened the attackers' appetite.

In each division of William's army the archers took post in front and advanced to about 100 yards of the foe. Behind them were heavy infantry, men in knee-length coats of chain mail – or in trousered overalls as depicted in the Bayeux Tapestry – and helmets with nose protectors, armed with long swords and shields, and behind them, ready to exploit any breach in the line, came the flower of the army, the colourful and well trained cavalry contingents, also wearing chain armour and able to make full use of their swords and lances because of an invention long adopted on the Continent but ignored in England, the stirrup.

A trumpet clarion announced the start of battle, whereupon the archers let fly their arrows uphill at the English. Most appear to have gone over their heads or into their shields. Next, the minstrel knight Ivo Taillefer gave a performance of juggling with lance and sword in front of the English, then spurred his horse deep into their ranks and was hacked to death. Then the infantry laboured up the hill with cavalry in close support. Pelted with a crude miscellany of missiles, they received a battering on the objective by axe, club, and spear, which easily penetrated their bodies through their chain mail. The whole French line wavered, and certainly on the left the Bretons broke and fled; they of course could expect as little mercy from Norman chroniclers as from the motley of fyrd and housecarls who pursued them down the hill, yelling their battle cry, 'Out! Out!' The Breton cavalry went headlong into the bog (where the pond can be seen) and suffered awful slaughter as their horses foundered.

This might have been Harold's moment, the moment at which to give full rein to the ferocious attacking power of his housecarls, which provided him with his one hope of victory. But there was danger in attacking too early, and Harold was well acquainted with the tactic, first practised by the Danes, of feigning flight in order to throw the pursuers off balance. It appears that one or both of his brothers' housecarls went after the Bretons, and a tremor of panic shook the Normans too, sped by the report that William was slain. But Harold held his hand. Through the clamour of voices, raised in ardour, pain, and panic, one can imagine his, yelling for the recall of the men whose impetuosity was dissipating his force.

It was William who made decisive use of the crisis. His horse had been felled in the fighting, and hearing the rumour that he had himself been felled, he removed his helmet to show himself to his men and quickly organised an attack on the pursuers of the Bretons, leading his knights across the slope from right to left. As depicted in the Bayeux Tapestry, the English were surrounded on a mound, which must be the one visible (from our roadside viewpoint) beyond the pond, with a growth of broom upon it, as if unaltered by the passing of nine hundred years. Unaided by Harold, the men on the mound were isolated and wiped out, and it is probable that at least one of his brothers died here. Thus the defeat of the Bretons was more than redeemed by the Normans.

There was probably a long pause for reorganisation and the provision of remounts before the attack was resumed. The knights now led the onslaught, and a tremendous swiping match developed, with fearful slaughter of the wretched, unarmoured cobs and with the English dead remaining upright in their ranks because there was no room to fall. The fighting was at its fiercest on what is now Abbey Farm, just short of the remains of the Abbey, and it is sickening to contemplate the sludge of blood and writhing carnage spread over these few acres of ground; Senlac the hill came to be called, supposedly because of the sand-stream or sand-lake at its foot, but some say the word is derived from *sanguelac* or blood-lake. William apparently lost another horse but there was no sagging of his leadership.

However, the Normans fell back, and again part of the English force pursued them, only themselves to be struck down by a fresh wave of attackers. According to the account written on William's behalf by William of Poitiers (a priest who was not present at the battle), the retreat was a feigned one, in the manner taught by the Danes on foot. But it is not easy to see how horsemen could achieve this manoeuvre when careering downhill away from a scene of horror. All that is certain is that William had inspired his knights to combine courage with cohesion and that Harold once again lost control of his troops when a concerted counter-attack might just have saved his kingdom from toppling over the abyss. Maybe his great and continuous exertions during the past five weeks had blunted his powers of decision and obliged him to fight what William of Poitiers described as 'a battle of a new type: one side vigorously attacking; the other resisting as if rooted to the ground'.

Showing as much flexibility as determination, William now organised a better coordinated attack, ordering his archers to fire high trajectory, thus making their arrows harder to shield, while his foot and horsemen made a combined assault, after further pause for replenishment of weapons, horses, and courage. This, according to Norman legend, which must be based on eyewitness report, achieved the result desired. An arrow landed in Harold's eye. He plucked at it, broke its shaft, but could not extract it, and in his agony he dropped his axe. Sensing victory, the attackers massed and hacked down the forlorn human wall surrounding the standard of Wessex. Four knights are said to have spotted the prostrate form of Harold and to have ingloriously plunged their swords into it. English sources refer only to the fact of his death, in words such as Florence of Worcester's: 'About twilight, the king, alas, fell.'

His brothers, Gyrth and Leofwine, had also fallen, and by exerting pressure round both flanks, William almost surrounded the remains of the disheartened and desperately weary troops who still fought for England. They fell back, the fyrd in flight, the housecarls still fighting. The knights pursued them over Caldbec Hill and on towards the forest at mounting speed, but in their haste and in the gloaming of evening they failed to spot a ravine concealed by undergrowth, to which the deep-sunk brook that runs under the roads at 744177 and 743170 screams its claim to identity. Many horses fell in, and many riders were killed or badly injured. Now the indomitable housecarls came to life again and inflicted further loss and anguish on the impetuous Normans. William, who had lost his third horse, ordered yet another attack, and only when the sounds of battle receded into the great forest did he sound the retreat and rally his men on Caldbec Hill (the name of which is not, however, derived from Called Back). It was now dark. Leaving his troops to their fitful dreams, William set up his pavilion at the place where the corpses lay at their thickest, around Harold's standard. There he cheerfully ate meat. Not until daylight did the full horror of the carnage on the hillside reveal itself.

Having attended to the burial of his friends and vowed to build an abbey on the ground where Harold fell, William waited five days, hoping that the surviving English chieftains would arrive to make submission, as they had done to Caesar. Disappointed in this, he resolved to capture London, not by the Roman road through the Andredsweald and Rochester but by the more circuitous route through East Kent, thus showing appreciation of the need to secure the main gateway into England and perhaps realisation that the route through the forest was vulnerable to raids by guerrillas. The remnant of the defeated army was already lurking there, and so too were many fugitives from the terror that had been deliberately spread by the Normans before the battle. William well knew the difficulty of winkling them out.

His first objective was Romney, and here he inflicted vengeance on the people for the slaying of the Normans who had landed there. His method of doing this has to be left to the imagination. All that is known is that its effect was highly salutary, for he encountered not a spark of defiance during his further journeying through Kent; indeed the folk are said to have flocked to make submission 'like flies settling on a wound'. The surrender of Dover was presented to him by the leading burghers, and he showed awareness of its importance by staying there eight days in order to build fortifications. Oddly enough at William's bidding, Harold had put a palisade and earthwork round the church built by the Saxons next the Roman lighthouse. William strengthened the palisade and constructed further earthworks. He then went to Canterbury and stayed there a month. His aim was to win the confidence of the people, and he was willing enough to allow the inhabitants of Kent to retain their laws and customs, one of which, named Gavelkind, was to the advantage of any usurper, for it required a dead man's land to be divided equally among his sons and thus impeded the acquisition of property and power by a single person. As for the Church, William had no wish to quarrel with any vicar of the Pope. However, Archbishop Stigand of Canterbury had retired to London.

William set out for London towards the end of November. He reached Southwark without difficulty but found the Londoners waiting defiantly behind their wall, having declared for a juvenile scion of the house of Alfred, Edgar The Aethling. Indeed, so defiant was their mood that they made a sortie across London Bridge as the Normans approached. This was beaten back with heavy loss, but William was deterred from making an assault crossing. He instead reverted to the policy of spreading terror and famine, thus isolating the Londoners. Having started by setting fire to Southwark, he laid waste, with frightening speed and thoroughness, to a belt on either side of the Thames as far as Wallingford, in Oxfordshire. Stigand, Archbishop of Canterbury, turned up here and swore fealty to William. He appears to have been a crafty customer, for the story was put about, and long accepted as truth, that he had surprised and staggered William during his march on London by equipping an army with the branches of Swanscombe Wood (TQ 6073). So alarmed was William by the sight of this moving forest, so the story goes, that when Stigand stepped from it, threatening an immediate attack, he at once granted him the concession that Kent should retain her ancient liberties. The myth is perpetuated in the motto displayed by the County of Kent beneath Horsa's White Horse, *Invicta.* It is of unsound warranty.

Soon after Stigand's defection, Edgar The Aethling came to Berkhamstead to make submission, together with many other notabilities, including the leading men of London. Although William duly received an oath of loyalty from them, he still did not take the fall of London for granted and continued to lay waste the country as he returned towards the city from the north-west. There is a report in one of the Norman accounts (that of Jumiège) of a fight with the citizens outside the city walls, and another (that of Guy of Amiens) mentions preparations for a siege and negotiations with the garrison commander. But such resistance as there was could not have been more than brief and desultory. William gained an entry, as Roman, Saxon, and Danish invaders had done before him, and as none would do again. On Christmas Day he was consecrated King of England in Westminster Abbey. The Archbishop of York officiated.

Dover c.1600

Chapter 7

THE CASTLES

Although the Saxons had their burhs, their means of defence were primitive, offering no prospect of counter-attack until the mobilisation and arrival of the main army. The new Norman king demanded a more advanced and elaborate system, and he implemented it with urgent awareness of the danger of an invasion by the Danes and of an uprising within. His system was elementary in itself, that of placing castles on features of strategic importance. They filled both the defensive role of securing such features and of giving refuge when needed to the local people and their herds, and the offensive one of housing sufficient troops to dominate the countryside as far as the area of the next castle. They were built on the motte and bailey principle, the motte being a mound forming the kernel of the defence, the bailey the outworks, surrounded by wall, bank, or ditch, or all three. There could be many elaborations on this design.

A few castles of supreme importance remained under the direct control of the King. Most were built and manned under the feudal system, by which barons and knights undertook responsibilities for defence in exchange for the award or retention of large estates. It was with the promise of such awards that the Norman noblemen had fought so hard at Hastings, and the whole of Sussex and a large part of Kent were duly divided among them.

In the early years of their conquest the Normans built castles of wood surrounded by wooden palisades. However, William wanted something special for London, as much no doubt to overawe its inhabitants as any external foe. He therefore built a huge stone castle-keep, 30 yards square — the Tower of London — on a mound (which may have originated as an earthwork) on the marsh by the river just outside the south-east corner of the Roman wall. This great monument of conquest was completed at about the same time as the Conqueror's life, in 1087, and it must indeed have inspired great awe, rising stark and domineering, high above the wall and the wooden shack houses inside it. Surrounded initially by a modest bailey, the Tower excited the interest of almost all of William's Norman and Plantagenet successors and received frequent additions. Henry III (1216-72) built a curtain wall with many towers and gave the main keep the name of White Tower by having it lime-washed, and Edward I (1272-1307) built a great rampart wall as an extra curtain, in accordance with the new pattern of concentric defence. An interior addition in 1692 turned the Tower into the Army's main storehouse and armoury, and after its destruction by fire, two barrack blocks were built in 1845, adding yet further complexity to what originated as a fort of great simplicity.

The Normans made use of the Roman wall round London and subsequently enlarged it. A good example of their work is on display behind Midland House, 8-10 Cooper's Row (standing on Tower Hill on the northern side of Trinity Square), and although the lower 13 feet of Roman wall is 1,000 years older than the 22 feet of medieval wall that rise above it, interspersed by archers' loops, it is hard to see the divide between the old and the less old. Another interesting example is preserved in St Alphage's Garden, EC2, which is just to the north of and parallel to the street named London Wall and adjacent to the modern mock fortifications of the Barbican. Here the combined Roman-medieval defence wall is topped by red-brick crenellations added in 1476.

Apart from the Tower, the only castle in the South-East still retained as a Royal one is that of Dover. Its first Constable appointed by William was his half-brother, Odo, Bishop of Bayeux, who was also made Earl of Kent as reward for his part in the Battle of Hastings, the pictorial record of which is thought to have been woven by the people of Canterbury before being transferred to Odo's home see, Bayeux. Grasping and overbearing, Odo rapidly made himself so unpopular that the leading men of Kent went to the extraordinary length of inviting Count Eustace of Boulogne to seize the earldom — the man who had had the fight with the people of Dover in 1051 and had subsequently been badly wounded on Caldbec Hill near the end of the battle, for which he also received a holding in Kent, though only a small one. Eustace duly answered the call, arriving from Boulogne at a convenient moment, when William was away on a visit to Normandy and Odo, left in charge by William, had been drawn north of the Thames to quell a rebellion. The rebellious men of Kent gave Eustace a great welcome at Dover, and without waiting for promised reinforcements they together launched an attack on the Castle. It beat in vain against the defenders of the palisaded hill-top and dissolved in an ignominious scuttle when the defenders switched to an attacking role and chased their would-be assailants into the sea or across the valley. Eustace made a breathless escape and returned to Boulogne.

Two years later (1069) the Danes made a last appearance off the coast of Kent, being seen from Dover and Sandwich. They were driven off by means which are not recorded but may again be connected with the aggressive spirit of the men in the Castle. Certainly they achieved better results than their Saxon predecessors, and perhaps this is why over a hundred years passed before the wooden fort on this peak of such obvious importance was exchanged for a fine and massive keep, 95 feet high, built by Henry II between 1181 and 1187. Still in excellent condition, this stands on a subsidiary, further inland mound to that adorned by those incongruous guardians of the key feature, the Roman lighthouse and the Saxon church. The elaborate wall supporting the fortress hill replaced the palisades shortly before the building of the keep, and the formidable, deep-sided outer curtain wall was built a few years after the siege of 1216, of which more will be said as the story unfolds. Further extensions were made in the 16th and 17th Centuries, only to be demolished in favour of an outer ring of earthworks, connected by underground passages, constructed to repel Napoleon. Barracks on the south side, of which the officers' mess remains dominant and serene, and a battery emplacement on the east were added in the 19th Century, and further additions, mainly subterranean, were made in 1940.

There can surely be no other castle that has played such an enduring part in the defence of Britain, and it is entirely appropriate that a serving soldier should still occupy the barbican house of the Constable's Gate, being the commander of Shorncliffe and Dover Garrison; he holds the appointment of Deputy Constable, the Constable being the Lord Warden of the Cinque Ports. Dover Castle remains very much alive, although maintained as an ancient monument by the Department of the Environment. It makes vivid impact when seen from the Channel, as by a prospective invader, or glimpsed as a magic eyrie on the approach from Folkestone on A20 or from Canterbury on A2 as far back as Lydden Hill (2545).

Linking Dover with London were the episcopal cities of Canterbury and Rochester, and the defences of both received the attention of the Norman kings. It is stated in Domesday Book (1086) that eleven houses had been built in Canterbury's defence ditch, which tells of a familiar pattern of erosion. It is not known what the Normans did about it, or what improvements they made to the wall that had been scaled by the Danes back in 1011, for their work has been obscured by the extensive elaborations made under the goad of a threatened invasion in the late 14th Century. Seventeen of the twenty-two turrets built then remain, and thanks to recent clearance work, a considerable stretch of the southern wall is on view, while the magnificent West Gate, with its twin turrets, still admits incoming traffic. Henry Yeveley was diverted from working on the Cathedral nave to design the fortifications, and he appears to have been the first Englishman to envisage the use of firearms, the development of which was in its crudest infancy. His foresight can be seen in the roundness of the turrets, which are sited to provide mutually supporting crossfire, and in the loopholes for handguns, shaped like upturned keyholes. No doubt the work met with the approval of the Knight of the Shire, Sir Geoffrey Chaucer, who as Clerk of the King's works from 1389-91 had to devote as much time to defence projects as to poetry.

The one visible Norman contribution to the defence of Canterbury is the castle, which was one of the earliest built and had a large keep, standing just inside the Roman wall on the south-west corner of the perimeter (143574). It is hard to know why it was put there, for the south-east and the north-west were the most likely lines of approach by an enemy. It was to acquire no distinction as a centre of resistance and is much dilapidated.

Rochester has a castle of great distinction, which from 1392 to 1856 directly overlooked the bridge over the Medway, the present one having been built 60 yards further downriver. Developed in three stages under royal instigation, it was completed with the building of its splendid keep – 70 feet square and 125 feet high – between 1127-39 and entrusted to the Archbishop of Canterbury. The keep still stands serene, despite its battering in two sieges (described in Chapter 9), and so do parts of the curtain wall, including the north-west bastion. Like Canterbury's, but to more obvious purpose, this castle was built in the south-west corner of the old perimeter wall, which also received medieval embellishments, only a few of which remain.

To make sure that the heights between Dover and Lympne were in good keeping, William entrusted this part to the feudal care of one of his most distinguished soldier-knights, Hugh de Montfort. He established his castle at Saltwood (1635 – PO), which stands in a re-entrant on the slopes above Hythe and was better supplied with water from the stream than today. There may have been an old encampment here, and maybe some of the massive digging that preceded the building of the bailey walls was done before the arrival of the Normans. The castle is in good repair, and its fine twin-towered gatehouse (built in 1380) is still lived in. However, it has gained more notoriety than fame, having served as the assembly point for the murderous assault on Archbishop Thomas Becket.

There are two ranges of hills in this area. One runs inland from the cliffs between Dover and Folkestone and forms a ridge overlooking Folkestone. The importance of its most prominent spur, Castle Hill (2137), was recognised probably well before the coming of the Romans, and the clear and simple remains of a Norman motte and bailey, without stone embellishment, show that it was recognised by de Montfort. The other range, forming just as steep a ridge, runs westward from Hythe forming the border of the Romney Marsh. The Normans built a church here at Lympne (1234) overlooking the remains of Stutfall Castle, and there seems certain to have been a fort alongside it, although the castle that can be seen there (PO) was apparently not built (for the Archdeacon of Canterbury) until 1360.

Further northwards in Kent, Chilham (0653 – PO) stands on a spur along which the trackway to Canterbury runs and has a tradition of military history dating from the Roman occupation. This fell within the gift of Odo, and the work of his tenant or heir can be seen in the interesting octagonal keep that stands on a stone platform of great strength and apparent antiquity. It gives a greater impression of strength and dominance than the Jacobean castle adjacent to it.

Just as Chilham dominates the valley of the Stour, so Eynsford (TQ 5465 – DoE) dominates that of the Darent. This was given to William's first Norman Archbishop of Canterbury, Lancfranc, and he was spurred to fortification by the predatory ambition of his rival, Odo. The original construction was of a watch tower, which being by the riverline had to be high, and to protect it a great curtain wall was built, starting as early as around 1088. The castle has been in ruin for over six centuries, and its main interest is in the example it provides of Norman architecture in its rugged original. Parts of the wall remain near their full height of 30 feet and can be seen to derive their strength from the remarkable cohesion binding and aligning the rough chunks of flint, sometimes in the pattern of a herring-bone.

Further inland a knight named Crevecoeur was granted the Saxon stronghold of Leeds Castle (8353) on the River Len. It was acquired, two centuries later, by that inveterate builder King Edward I, who greatly developed it and gave it its watery surrounds as much for pleasure as for defence. It retains its idyllic appearance, which the public have had the chance to relish only since 1976.

The valley of the Medway westwards from what is now Maidstone was entrusted to another of William's lieutenants at Hastings, Richard de Fitz-Gilbert. He established his castle at the point controlling the main crossing place and route of access into the Andredsweald, and he converted his name to its name, Tonbridge. The Saxons had established a burh on a mound overlooking the river (5846 – DC), and Richard enlarged this mound by the use of men and baskets and fortified it as his motte. He built a bailey adjoining it on the south-east side, to which the massive gatehouse, with its quadruple towers and double portcullis, was added in the 13th Century. The motte, standing next to it, is now a jungle of trees and undergrowth.

Sussex was divided into six strips of land running northward from the sea, which were given the peculiar name of rapes. They were granted to well trusted Normans, of whom the only one not to have served at Hastings, Roger de Montgomery, received the largest chunk, consisting of the rapes both of Chichester and Arundel. The walls of Chichester were strengthened and a castle built inside their south-east corner, but this was demolished in 1217, when probably still made of wood, and nothing remains of it except a grassy mound in Priory Park. A castle built on the hill overlooking Midhurst (SU 889215) was also soon abandoned.

Arundel (TQ 0107 – PO), however, has maintained a fine record of durability. Standing on a natural platform 4 miles inland, it overlooked what in Norman times was the estuary of the River Arun and had already been used as a burh by the Saxons. The beauty of its surroundings and the magnificence of its subsequent development, which continued in castellated style well into the 19th Century, is apt to divert attention from the simplicity of the original concept. This can be seen in the central mound, which is obviously artificial, and the square part of the keep upon it, combined with the square interior of the double barbican. It would appear that the keep formed part of the bailey wall; an eccentric arrangement.

The next rape eastwards was granted to William de Braose, and rather than occupy one of the peaks that had served of old as hillforts he chose a valley controlling access into the interior from off the Downs, being guided no doubt by the importance of water supply. The remains of his castle can be seen at Bramber (186107 – NT) next the River Adur. There is a certain rugged defiance about the jagged edge of what is left of the keep and about the steepness of the climb up from the moat.

The next rape eastwards was assigned to William de Warenne, and he too concentrated on the defence of a river line at the point where it begins to carve its passage through the Downs, in this instance the River Ouse at Lewes, under the lee of the long fortified Mount Caburn. Lewes had become an important settlement of the Saxons, and de Warenne sought to dominate it by constructing his own precipitous hill inside the town, by the enforced haulage of chalk blocks. He built two mounds in this manner, the prominence of which can best be discerned from Offham Hill (3911) on the north-west side of the town. The wall of the keep is flush with the side of its artificial cliff, and it comes dramatically into view at close quarters for the visitor who turns northwards into Castle Gate Street off the High Street. The circular structure of flint and Caen stone, of which the walls of the keep are made, was not put up until the end of the 11th Century, replacing a wooden structure. Two projecting towers were added about a hundred years later, and the barbican or outer gateway through which the street runs dates from the 14th Century.

Like most castles built in towns by the Normans, Lewes Castle had only a short history of occupation, falling into decay in 1347 for the simple reason that the de Warenne family became extinct. After a while people crept in and chipped out pieces of stone and other material that might be useful. They no doubt did this with a certain atavistic relish, for while the Normans regarded the castles as shields against invaders, the inhabitants saw them as symbols of their subjugation, the strongholds from which the usurpers rode forth and exacted taxation from them.

The next rape was granted to William's half-brother, Count Robert of Mortain, and whereas the castles to the west of his rape were all sited well inland, he was more restricted by the Andredsweald and chose their original landing place, Pevensey. Not until the 12th Century was the building of a stone structure begun inside the walls of the Romans' Anderida Castle. It was of advanced design, with inner and outer wards and a raised cylindrical keep, but it can be seen to have endured rather less well than the Roman walls forming its bailey.

The sixth of the Sussex rapes, that of Hastings, went to Count Robert of Eu, and he already had a castle of Norman origin available, the collapsible fort brought from Normandy and installed as its second site on the cliff-sided promontory (8209 – DC) that had more sea around it than today. The stone walls that eventually replaced it still stand but it is not certain that the keep, which was planned to be built in 1172, was ever completed. From the 13th Century onwards it was used more for religious than defensive purposes.

Guildford and Reigate formed the pivots for the domination of the North Downs and routes running southwards from them. Guildford had long contained a royal residence and ranked as a borough with its own mint. Its castle (999493 – DC) is on the south side of the town, overlooking the River Wey, and provides a marvellous example of Norman skill and industry, for the keep stands on a spur artificially detached from Pewley Hill and considerably enlarged. Although gaunt and dilapidated, it is of formidable size, still rising in parts to its pristine 63 feet, and it was a great feat to have built such a structure, in the early 12th Century, on a mound designed to bear a mere wooden tower and palisade. Its bailey wall, through which the Castle Arch gateway was made in 1256, confined a large area in which the buildings included a palace often used by various kings. Others allowed it to fall into decay, and the castle contained few of its old glories when sold by King James I in 1611.

Reigate, like Lewes, came within the domain of the de Warennes, Earls of Surrey. A castle was built on the mound (251503) below the Downs, and the town grew up around it, probably in the 12th Century. The castle was completely demolished by order of Parliament as a result of a rising that flickered briefly at the end of the Civil War in July 1648. A public park has emerged from this massive task of destruction. Nine miles eastwards, by Bletchingley (3250), stood another Norman castle of which nothing is left but a few ruins. This had been built by de Clare, of Tonbridge, and it suffered severe pillage at royalist hands when de Clare fought for de Montfort in 1264. (See page 75.)

Controlling access to the North Downs from the west, near the foot of the Hog's Back, stood a manor that had long been and remained the property of the Bishop of Winchester. Soon after the Norman conquest he turned it into a castle, which took the name of Farnham (SU 837473 – DoE) from the market town it overlooks. It consisted initially of a square tower built on an artificial mound, inside a compound bounded by bank and ditch and subsequently a curtain wall. During the 12th Century the tower was demolished, it would appear as punishment for a visit to France made by the Bishop without the King's permission. Instead of replacing it, the Bishop encased the mound with a wall and rectangular built-in turrets. He thus built a most unusual type of keep, parts of which still stand at their pristine 37 feet, in contrast with other parts that were lowered by Roundheads as the punishment known as 'slighting' for the castle's brief occupation by Royalist troops. Another feature, in excellent condition, is the incongruous redbrick entry tower built in the 15th Century.

Such was the main framework of castle-defence instituted by the Normans in the South-East counties. Many additions were made to it, mainly through the urge of anxious Englishmen to turn their homes into castles, by adding crenellations or battlements. This practice was apt to rouse the suspicions of any king who was unsure of the loyalty of all his subjects, and after Henry II had come to the throne in 1154 he made it conditional on the issue of a 'licence to crenellate'. Among those for which successful application was made were Hever Castle (TQ 4745 – PO) in 1274 and Allington Castle (7557 – PO) in 1281. The latter could provide an important link in the overall defence scheme, standing as it does on the west bank of an eastward bulge in the Medway, midway between Rochester and Leeds Castles.

Prolonged war with France during the 14th Century brought royal encouragement for the fortifying of houses in places of importance, and the licence for Bodiam (7825 – NT), issued to the veteran warrior Sir Edward Dallingrigge in 1385, gives as its purpose 'defence of the adjacent country and resistance to our enemies'. It stands on the River Rother, 10 miles inland, and is a marvel of a massive fortified barrack, over 100 feet square, with a wide apron of water all round it. Unlike the Norman castle-compounds, this is a single fortress, capable of a great volume of arrow projection from the various levels of its closely spaced towers, and the possessor at one time of a 15-inch bombard, one of the earliest of all artillery pieces, which was found in its moat and is now in the Rotunda Museum, Woolwich. Another feature of this castle is that the quarters are so arranged to facilitate the isolation of any part of the garrison that might turn mutinous. Still in excellent condition, the castle was given to the National Trust by Lord Curzon, who described it as 'the most fairy of English castles'.

Sussex contains another gem a few miles westwards in Herstmonceux Castle (6410) which is now part of the Royal Observatory but can be seen at certain times. This too is something of a fairy castle, being made of lovely soft-red brick and having a variety of flat-sided and round towers, all in excellent condition, surrounded by a moat. It dates from 1446, and containing a large, still used domestic complex, its impression is more of a barracks of great beauty than of a stronghold of great importance. Standing on the edge of the Pevensey Levels, its site had gained value from the thinning of the Andredsweald.

Even the mouth of the Thames was proved to be open to French raiders, and in 1380 Lord Cobham was authorised to convert a manor house at Cooling (753760) into a castle to drive off any marauding party that might land on the estuary bank. Some of the turrets of the wall remain, including a very fine double-towered gateway, designed by Yeveley of Canterbury fame, and inside them are a farm and private house. The walls of a keep or court can also be seen, approached by a right-angled turn beyond moat and gateway, designed to remove the impetus from any rush.

It is fortunate that Cooling survived the Great Civil War, for the Cobhams were staunch Royalists, and their castle at Starborough (just inside Surrey, 4244, a few miles west of Hever) was among three ordered to be made indefensible after a rising in 1648. Permission to fortify it had been granted in 1341, and presumably it was selected for what amounted to destruction, with plenty of loot for those carrying out the task, because Cobham had made it so formidable. The moat remains, so do foundations of its curtain wall and four round towers.

The biggest and most thorough task of destruction carried out by Cromwell's men was of a castle built by King Edward III around 1350. He named it Queenborough in honour of his Queen Philippa, and it stood on the Isle of Sheppey at the mouth of the Swale, overlooking what was then the island's one harbour and controlling entrance up the Medway. (Its scant remains lie on the west side of the railway station at 913722, not where marked Moat in the same map square.) It was of great strategic importance and of great strength, being concentric in design, thus confronting the attacker with a fresh obstacle at every turn. It must also have been attractive, being a frequent magnet of royal patronage. Maybe Cromwell ordered its demolition in 1650 more through fear of its falling into the hands of raiders than through vengeance. Only a few bumps are left, testifying to the zeal with which a massive task of dismantling was carried out.

RYE AND ROMNEY

Estimate of coastline in 1066, with existing coastline and rivers shown by briefly broken lines (with acknowledgement to Thomas Lewin, 1862). Places of origin after 1066 are shown in italics. Contour marking at 100 feet.

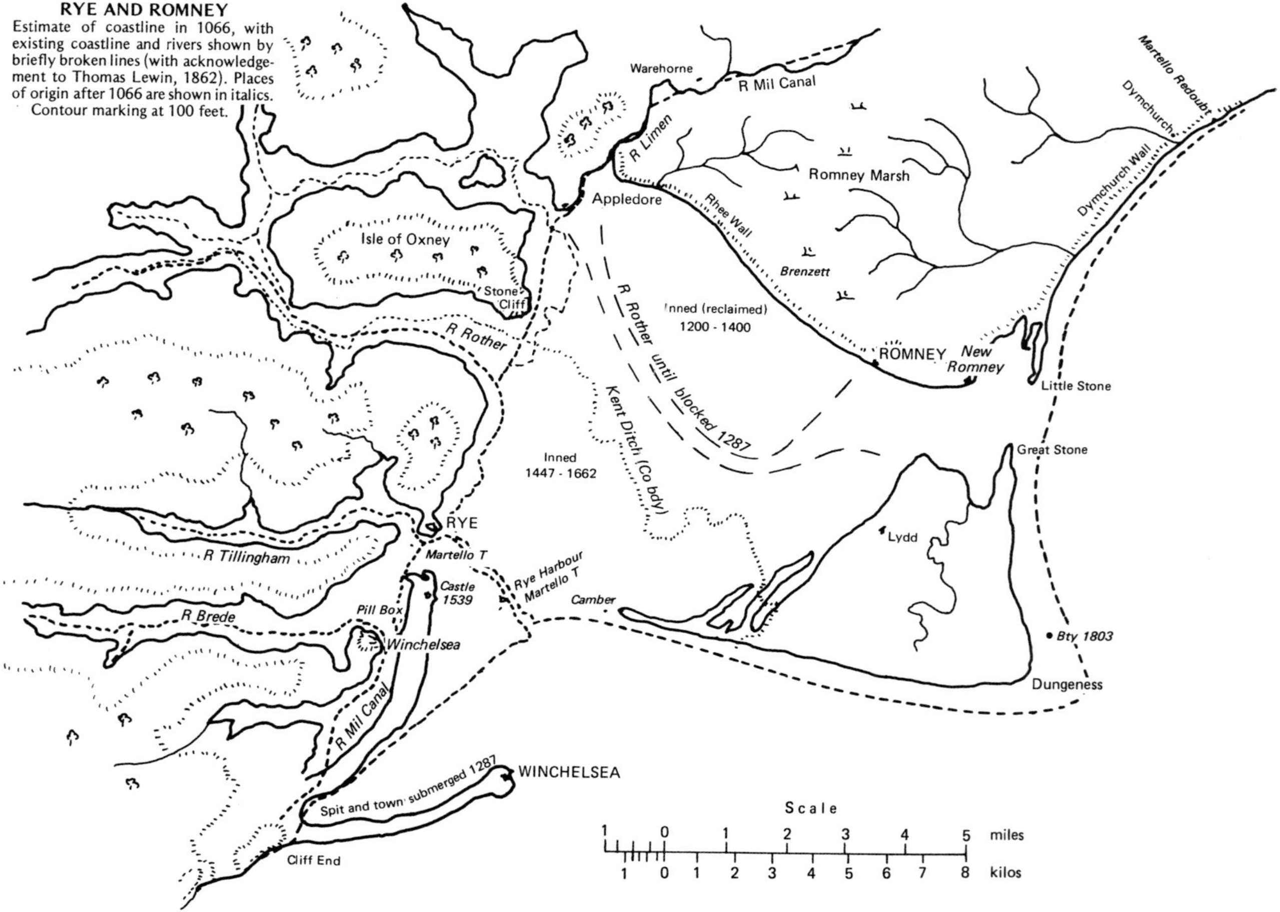

Chapter 8

THE CINQUE PORTS

The concept of the Cinque Ports, but not the name, originated from Edward The Confessor. He had been put to much expense and anxiety in keeping a fleet at readiness to repel an invasion long threatened by King Magnus of Norway. The danger subsided with the death of Magnus in 1047, and although raiding Norsemen made a number of landings the following year, in which they plundered Sandwich once again but were repulsed from Thanet, Edward decided in 1050 that he no longer had need of a standing navy, and he took the drastic step of disbanding it. As a substitute he made arrangements with the ports of Sandwich, Dover, Fordwich (up to which the Stour formed an estuary), and Romney that they should provide him with men and ships when required, in exchange for the profits of justice in their courts. A similar type of arrangement was undoubtedly made with Hastings and Hythe, and it was in fulfilment of their contract that ships from these six ports rallied to the call of Harold in 1066.

The grant of favours in return for service was of the very essence of the Conqueror's system of rule, and just as he arranged for the defence of the land by dividing it among his henchmen, so he entrusted the defence of the sea approach to the five ports of Kent and Sussex (leaving out Fordwich). They were to form the shield behind which a larger fleet might be mobilised for war, and they were given concessions, rather than money, for this service. These concessions steadily accrued over the years and put the Ports in an extraordinarily privileged position. They were freed from the strangulating web of taxation exacted under such intriguing headings as lastage, tallage, passage, kayage, rivage, ponsage, wreck, and lovecope; their courts, from which they continued to draw the profits of justice, or sac and soc, were made independent from the county courts; they were given the right of den and strond, which was a great asset to their peacetime trade of fishing and the cause of great jealousy, for it allowed them to land and sell their fish at Great Yarmouth; and their freemen were all given the mode of address (but not the title) of baron and were granted the coveted 'honour at court' of holding the canopy over the king and queen at coronations. The Warden of the Cinque Ports was a royal officer, responsible only to the King, and had the difficult task of instilling proper respect for this royal master among men who had long been in the habit of indulging in piracy to supplement their earnings from fishing.

Although the name of Cinque Ports probably came into use during the reign of the Conqueror, its first entry into a known document is in a charter of Henry II, about 1155. Here it is laid down that the Ports had to supply fifty-seven ships for fourteen days each year, when notified by the King, and with payment for any longer service if required; each ship to be manned by twenty-one men and a boy, which would presumably be rather more than required for its normal function of fishing. (Pictures show that conversion from fishing smack to warship was achieved by the placing of castellated structures on the bows, stern, and masthead, the large square sail serving for either purpose.) A list dated 1229 gives the distribution of the fifty-seven as follows: Hastings 21, Romney 5, Hythe 5, Dover 21, Sandwich 5.

It is surprising that Sandwich should have made such a small contribution. This was the leading commercial port of England, and time and again it had been chosen as the assembly place on the mobilisation of the King's navy. This function it was to retain, and in 1324 it was allotted two keepers of the port, as 'on account of its ample size a very large number of vessels can put in at the same time and this is a danger to the town'. The danger had a long history of fulfilment, yet in shameful contrast with nearby Richborough, the defences long remained woefully inadequate. Indeed, the earliest record of fortifications is of earthworks and barricades thrown up by the townsmen in 1274-5 in revolt against unpopular measures, and these they were compelled to level and demolish. The existing earthworks, known in different parts as The Butts, Rope Walk, and Mill Wall, forming a raised promenade, were put up in the late 14th Century, together with barbican gates, of which the surviving one on the side of the port was reconstructed in Tudor times. Further measures were taken in the 15th Century, but as will be seen from later chapters, they could not keep out the French. Certainly the

French found Sandwich as rewarding an objective as had the Danes; indeed no place has a longer history of being successfully raided. It might perhaps have been better fortified if it had not been in the possession of the Archbishop of Canterbury.

Although all the Ports were equal in status, Dover was of the greatest importance, as its contribution shows. Its main function, when the King's enemies were quiescent, was the passage across the Channel of royal personages and stores. A defence wall, of which only basic traces remain, was built in the 14th Century, extending south-westwards from the Roman wall to a harbour that had shifted in this direction to the inlet used today as a basin. The Castle provided its surest defence.

Hythe had been developed as a replacement for the Roman port of Lympne, and it too suffered erosion from silting, to which tremendous momentum was given by some storms of great violence in and around 1284, when all the harbours of the Cinque Ports were bombarded both by the waves and by tons of shingle. Romney was hurled into extinction as a port by these storms, and all that remains of its ancient distinction is its fine old Saxon-Norman church (TR 0325), standing on land once reclaimed from the sea by great exertion and now 3 miles from it. New Romney was used as a substitute but was soon fighting a losing battle against the retreat of the sea and now stands at least a mile inland without any connecting waterway. Nothing much was done to fortify Hythe or either of the Romneys.

Certainly the continually shifting contest between sea and coastline made the problem of defence a fluid one, and while the Romney Marsh was advancing towards Dungeness, the sea was gaining ground in what is now known as Rye Bay; the tide, battering from west or south-west, kept pushing the shingle along until it accumulated along the bank running westwards from Dungeness. This gave Rye closer access to the sea. As can be vividly observed, this town consists of old buildings huddled on a promontory of sandstone rock, which provides a natural stronghold against the advance of sea or human enemy. In Norman times this promontory ran into a wide inlet of water, the combined estuary of the Rivers Rother, Tillingham, and Brede, and at the mouth of the inlet, standing on a strip of coast running into the bay from the west, was the harbour of Winchelsea. Because the harbour of Hastings was becoming seriously diminished, Rye and Winchelsea were both co-opted as subordinate members of Hastings as from 1195. They soon acquired responsibility for more than half the twenty-one ships allotted to Hastings.

Sadly, the sea smote the sides of Winchelsea with such fury that a new site for the town was chosen, standing on a promontory of cliff to the west. Occupation of it was taken in 1292, during the final disintegration and submersion of the spit of land on which the old town stood. By use of the River Brede, beneath the cliff on the northern side, Winchelsea was still able to function as a port, and around 1336 both she and Rye were accorded full membership of the Cinque Ports. The title was lengthened, rather than altered, to the Cinque Ports and Two Antient Towns.

The contribution made by Winchelsea rose to be second only to Dover. As a consequence the town became a favourite objective of raiders, and in six or seven attempts during the 14th and 15th Centuries the French made an entry and committed cruel pillage, this despite the steep natural slopes and new perimeter wall surrounding the town. It is perhaps not surprising that little remains of the wall, except for three arched gateways, the Strand, Pipewell, and New Gate. The last-named springs a surprise, for it stands half a mile outside the village. This void vividly expresses the decline of a thriving and aggressive sea port to a somnolent, extremely picturesque village, which nevertheless still ranks as a town.

Rye's most interesting fortification stands in a commanding position on the coastal side and consists of a small square fort with a tower at each corner; it was built around 1250 and takes the name of Ypres Tower from a subsequent owner. This must have been part of the perimeter wall, of which little other trace remains except the fine Land Gate, an extremely solid construction dating from 1340, through which the traffic still passes. An extra storey was added to this gateway — after the French had sacked the town in 1377.

With its port battered to dereliction, Hastings led the way in co-opting the aid of other towns. After Rye and Winchelsea had gained full membership of the Cinque, others were recognised as Limbs, gaining a share of privileges, and eventually their number rose to twenty-six. Some were co-opted because they belonged to a baron of one of the Cinque; thus Bekesbourne, which lies east of Canterbury, far inland, provided one of the twenty-one ships for which Hastings and the Ancient Towns remained responsible. Hastings itself provided only three, under an order of 1359, with Pevensey, Bulverhythe, and Bekesbourne one each, Rye five, Winchelsea ten, and Grange (near Gillingham but owned from Hastings) providing oarsmen; Romney was responsible for four, with Lydd one; Hythe still for five; Dover for nineteen, with Folkestone one and Faversham (on the north coast of Kent) one; and Sandwich for five in conjunction with adjacent Stonar, Fordwich, Deal, and Sarre (on the west coast of the Isle of Thanet). The list of contributors varied from year to year, with total constant at fifty-seven ships, and each year the pleas from the original five, for a further easing of their burden, grew in volume.

The part the Cinque Ports played in the defence of the South-East will be recorded as the story unfolds. All that need be stated here is that their heyday came in the 13th Century, following the ejection of King John from Normandy. Having won a notable victory over the French, the Ports for years indulged in raiding the French coast, regardless of the official state of the peace. They also waged undeclared warfare with the seamen of Yarmouth, and this erupted into open aggression of great violence when they together formed an expedition against the French and landed at Sluys in 1297. From the spark set off by a street brawl, the Portsmen set fire to thirty-two of the ships from Yarmouth and killed over two hundred of their crews.

Amazingly, King Edward I could inflict no effective punishment for this outrage, and the arrogant, unrepentant Portsmen continued to wage piracy against their fellow-countrymen, drawing cries of protest from Cornwall, Dorset, and Hampshire. This undoubtedly speeded the decline of their influence and led slowly but inexorably to the withdrawal of their privileges, which had in any case been devalued by their need to reward the many assistants co-opted as limbs. An even stronger factor was the declining prosperity of the ports, caused largely by silting but also by lack of enterprise in developing trade. Even by 1341 both Romney and Hythe were threatened with loss of liberties for their inability to provide their quota, and this was followed by a loss of pride as the French increasingly gained mastery of the Channel. The Ports continued to make a contribution but it sank to a small part of the whole, and eventually only Dover, and to a far smaller extent Rye, were able to remain in operation as ports. Only one privilege was (and still is) retained by the barons, that of holding the canopy at coronations.

Yet the mystique has never been erased, and not only in the original Cinque Ports but also in most of their member towns their badge is proudly displayed, showing a hybrid in triplicate, lion in front, ship's prow behind. It was King Edward I, smarting maybe under the disgrace of the Sluys, who sought to combine responsibilities on land with those at sea by linking the post of Lord Warden with that of Constable of Dover Castle. Long after this post became purely nominal, it continued to be held by people of the highest distinction. The Duke of Wellington was among them, and he lived and died in the Lord Warden's official residence, the castle built by Henry VIII at Walmer (see Chapter 11) long after the fame of the Ports had begun its decline. In recent years the post has passed from Sir Winston Churchill to the great Australian, Sir Robert Menzies, and from him to Queen Elizabeth the Queen Mother.

Leaving Lewes Castle

Chapter 9

WARRING BARONS

The feudal system was a brittle form of rule, hingeing on the loyalty of the barons, and during the four hundred years that followed the death of the Conqueror the peace of England depended very largely on the authority the King could wield, which in turn depended on the strength of his character. There was trouble as soon as the Conqueror was buried (at Caen in September 1087), stemming from his division of Normandy, which he left to his eldest son Robert, from England, which he left to his second one, William Rufus. Although only just reinstated as Earl of Kent after being imprisoned for making an armed attempt to gain the Papacy (no less), the adventurous Odo seized Rochester Castle early in 1088 and declared for Robert. Roger de Montgomery (Arundel), Richard of Tonbridge, and his own brother, Robert, Count of Mortain (Pevensey), were among those who supported him.

William Rufus decided to strike at Tonbridge first. He quickly gained it, setting fire to the wooden castle and wounding Richard. He then marched on Rochester, whereupon Odo took horse (or possibly boat) for Pevensey, presumably in hope of stirring his brother Mortain to offensive action. Showing his father's flair for concentrated action, Rufus turned about and marched to lay siege to the mixture of woodwork and Roman wall of Anderida Castle, Pevensey. Odo and Robert Mortain surrendered after holding out for six weeks. Odo undertook to obtain the surrender of Rochester and was sent there under escort to do this. On his arrival at its walls the gates were opened – and out rushed some horsemen and grabbed the entire party. William had now to lay siege to Rochester. He put up blockhouses to deny access to the castle from either side and sent summons for men from all over England, to which 30,000 are said to have rallied. In due course Odo was again compelled to capitulate, under the stress of heat, hunger, and disease. There were yells of 'Bring halters!' when he and his knights emerged from the motley of ramparts on the hill. Rufus chose merely to banish them.

The peace was next disturbed in 1135, when death ended the firm and just rule of Rufus's brother Henry and left the crown in dispute between Henry's nephew Stephen and his daughter Maud, who was known to be his choice. Stephen was first on the scene from the Continent. Although unable to gain Dover Castle, he advanced to London and was consecrated king. But he lacked the strength to control the country, and it slid into civil war and anarchy.

Stephen's strongest ally was his fiery wife Matilda, and in 1138 she advanced into Kent with her foreign mercenaries and gained Dover Castle, whose Constable, John de Fiennes, had taken most of the garrison off to fight in the Midlands. In 1139 the equally fiery Maud (whose real name was also Matilda) arrived, accompanied by her half-brother Robert, Earl of Gloucester, and troops from her husband's province, Anjou. Leaving Dover Castle behind her as a lone island of resistance for King Stephen, she subdued the whole of Kent and entered London. Stephen meanwhile was laying siege to Lincoln. Gloucester's men pounced on him there, captured him, and incarcerated him, chained, in a dungeon at Bristol.

This must have looked like game and match to Maud – but Matilda refused to concede it. She raised an army in Kent and with zealous aid from the people of London drove Maud out. The raw but eager levies from Kent and London pursued her to Winchester and laid siege to the city. Maud escaped their clutch but Gloucester was caught, imprisoned in Rochester Castle, and in due course exchanged for Stephen. Maud continued the contest with reinforcements from France, and not until 1145, following the death of Gloucester, did she leave the kingdom in Stephen's possession. In January 1153 her son Henry Plantaganet staked his claim, landing at Dover with a reputation gleaming from the conquest of Normandy (at the age of 19) and with the troops that had won it for him. He swiftly launched an attack on the Castle and took it, ending its fourteen-year tenure by the troops of Queen Matilda and conceiving the project of building a great keep of stone and masonry. The fame of his troops gained them unimpeded progress through Kent, but rather than engage Stephen in battle, Henry settled for a promise of the succession, which was fulfilled on Stephen's death in 1154.

Being a man of powerful personality, tremendous energy, and of great possessions far across Europe, Henry II kept the barons quiet, and even when Archbishop Becket of Canterbury was murdered at his instigation he could ride the crisis without eruption of civil war. His son and successor, Richard I, diverted the energy of the barons to foreign adventures, going on crusade with thirty-four ships of the Cinque Ports. He met his death (in 1199) when engaged on the defence of Normandy, leaving the throne to his brother John, who in 1204 was driven out of Normandy by King Philip Augustus of France. This restored the insularity of England and in the long run would turn the barons of Norman origin into true Englishmen. But at the time they felt anger that it had been allowed to happen, and it was greatly increased by John's demands on their purses and by his prolonged conflict with the Pope, which ended in another humiliation.

By the time John made abject surrender to the Pope, in 1213, King Philip of France had prepared a great expedition to invade England on the Pope's behalf. He did not care to disband it just because John had given in, and it duly sailed. Showing sound strategic instinct, John had assembled an army on the Barham Downs (TR 2151) and a great fleet at Dover, reputedly of 500 sail, of which the Cinque Ports contributed barely a tenth. This fleet won a great victory somewhere in the North Sea, off Damme. John, unfortunately, was not prepared to leave it at that. He took the war to France in 1214 and was heavily defeated. The barons raged against him with increased fury.

On June 15, 1215, they obtained his signature to the Magna Carta. John responded by bringing over some mercenaries from Flanders, upon which John de Albiney raised the flag of revolt by seizing Rochester Castle with a force estimated at 95-140 knights, together with sergeants, crossbow-men, and other ranks. The huge, tall keep of this castle was now about eighty years old, and with its moat and bailey walls must indeed have appeared impregnable. John, who was well experienced in these matters, set about reducing it with great vigour, having made a surprise entry into the city on October 11 and forcing the garrison to man their defences before they had fully stocked themselves with provisions. Setting up his headquarters on Boley Hill, immediately south of the castle and on higher ground, he sent in a constant stream of arrows and of heavy stones hurled by catapult artillery engines. These gained him a breach in the bailey wall and forced the defenders back to the keep, on which the stones could make no impression. John turned from battering to mining, setting his men a tremendous task of tunnelling, supported by pit props. At last the props were fired by the ignition of the fat of forty pigs. The south-east corner of the keep collapsed, leaving permanent mark in the repair work necessitated by the shudder. Even so, the defenders held out for a further two or three days, until hunger forced them into surrender on November 30, the fiftieth day of the siege. John was persuaded to spare the rebel knights from execution, contenting his troops with the hanging of one (perhaps more) of their subordinates. Other unfortunates, kicked out by the defenders as unwanted, had been mutilated.

The barons now invited the King of France to come to their aid. John visited Dover and Sandwich to boost the loyalty of the Portsmen, but with no success. French ships swarmed across the Channel and disgorged their troops unopposed at Stonar, next Sandwich, on May 21, 1216. King Philip's son, Prince Louis The Dauphin, was in command. Accompanied by the barons and troops who had welcomed him, he made triumphant progress through Canterbury and Rochester, having gained their castles after only token fights, and onwards to London, where further barons paid him homage. But Dover Castle was in the staunch keeping of a loyal Constable, Hubert de Burgh, and a message arrived for Louis from his father and king that he could not be considered to have gained a secure foothold until this stronghold was reduced. Rather than advance on Winchester, where John was rallying his forces, Louis therefore turned back to deal with Dover. He found that the massive new keep which was encased by a single curtain wall, with an extension as far as the Saxon church, had a worthy defender, backed by 140 men-at-arms.

Louis began the siege of Dover Castle in mid-June. He had brought some great battering engines from France, and with these he breached the outer curtain wall on the northern side. The assault that followed was repulsed. He now tried mining, throwing up a great mound of earth beneath the walls on the south side as protection against the stones and darts that were constantly poured upon the besiegers. The miners found the foundations too firm, and just when Louis was forced to fall back on the accumulative effect of siege a band of horsemen galloped through his investing troops and swept in through Godwin's Gate (on the north-east side) with replenishment of food and munitions. On October 19 King John died. Louis sent Hubert the news under a flag of truce, accompanied by a demand for the Castle's surrender and a threat that he would hang him from its walls if he declined. Hubert retorted (according to the chronicler Mathew Paris) with the words: 'Let not Louis hope that I will surrender as long as I draw breath. Never will I yield to French aliens this Castle, which is the very key and gate of England!' This of course tallied with King Philip's assessment, and how Louis must have wished that he had ignored it. He withdrew his troops back to France for the winter, determined to return and renew the siege, even though the death of John had deprived him of his pretext.

He duly made his return on April 22, 1217, again landing at Stonar. There had been a change of mood in England, and this was shown by the resistance of the people of Sandwich. Louis harshly quelled it and set the town ablaze. He resumed the siege of Dover but it cannot have been conducted with great vigour, for when in August eighty French ships were sighted from the Castle Hubert was able to galvanise the Portsmen into sending forty ships against them, with their crews reinforced by his own men. The French ships were heading for the mouth of the Thames. The Portsmen caught them in the approach to North Foreland, off Sandwich, and swept down upon them, concentrating superior force first at one point then another. They closed, grappled under a barrage of arrows, poured forth a blinding cloud of lime powder, and rushed on board wielding axes, with

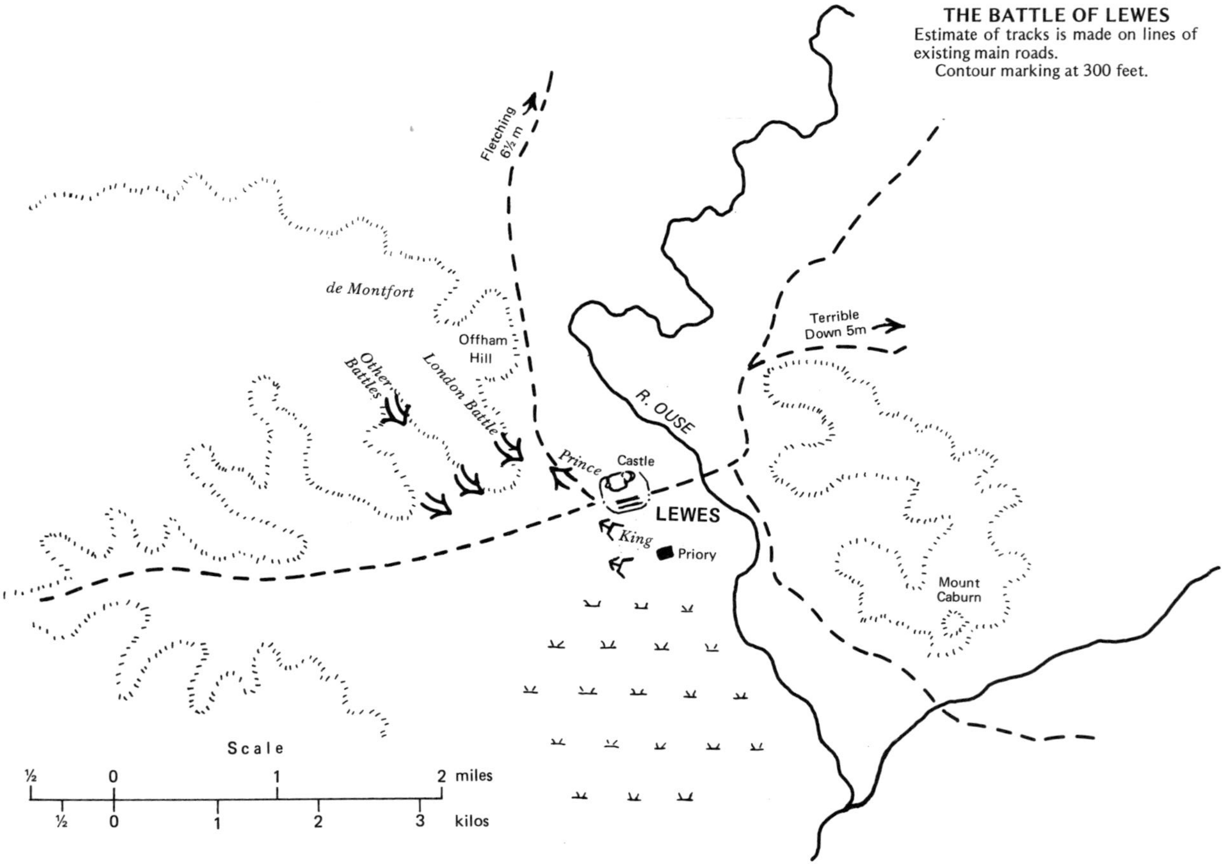

THE BATTLE OF LEWES
Estimate of tracks is made on lines of existing main roads.
Contour marking at 300 feet.

which they hacked both the bodies of their enemies and the riggings of their ships. The French fleet was slashed to pieces, and Louis was forced to make an ignominious retreat, sneaking back to France with his troops as best he could. It was the most famous victory ever gained by the combination of Castle and Ports.

This made an auspicious start to the reign of Henry III, the 9-year-old son of John. He gradually squandered it over the next forty-five years, most of all by the accumulation of foreigners in his entourage. Ironically, the opposition against him hardened around a Frenchman, the ascetic Simon de Montfort, who had married the King's sister and been made Earl of Leicester. A prolonged squabble over an extension of the Magna Carta, the Provisions of Oxford and Westminster, began to boil into armed conflict in June 1263. The barons raised the flag of revolt in Gloucestershire, and at the same time Sir Roger de Leybourne seized Dover Castle on their behalf. However, he changed sides in December, accepting the offer of the post of Constable of the Castle.

The King meanwhile had been virtually under siege in the Tower of London, and when his Queen tried to go by boat to Windsor, she was driven back by a barrage of stones and abuse from the people. The King summoned his retainers and moved out, keeping mobile court at Oxford, Winchester, and then Rochester. Finding he was not welcome at Dover, except without armed attendants, he moved sulkily to Windsor, having a brush en route at Southwark with Simon de Montfort, who would have been caught if the Londoners had not opened their gates and pulled him in.

In March 1264 the royalists cornered and captured a strong baronial force at Northampton, setting the war fully alight. From his base in London, Simon sought first to gain the whole of Kent. Dover Castle was seized, with the aid of the Portsmen and in the absence of de Leybourne, who had taken some of his troops to Northampton. But de Leybourne won the race for Rochester and established himself in the castle with powerful friends. The first attack was made on April 17, by the young Gilbert de Clare, Earl of Gloucester, from his castle at Tonbridge. This was thwarted by the firing of the suburbs on the south side. Next day, which was Good Friday, Simon advanced on the Medway bridge from London. After twice being repulsed, he somehow forced a crossing under the smoke and confusion caused by setting light to the bridge by use of a fire-ship. His men and de Clare's swarmed round the castle, committing pillage and sacrilege, and forced the garrison back from the bailey into the keep. However, a week later the King's army arrived, having covered the 150 miles from Nottingham in five days. Simon hurriedly withdrew his men to London, alarmed by a report of a royalist rising there, and the two armies avoided each other.

The royal troops now moved to Tonbridge and captured the castle before its owner, de Clare, could extract his troops from Rochester. They then tried to gain the Cinque Ports fleet but the ships put to sea at their coming, thus denying the King a link with friends in France. Leaving garrisons to secure Hastings and Pevensey castles, Henry then moved his weary men onwards through the hostile Andredsweald to the more defensible locality of Lewes, the owner of whose castle, John de Warenne, Earl of Surrey, was his brother-in-law and faithful ally. Being famed for his piety, Henry made the Priory of St Pancras (just south of Lewes at 498097) his headquarters and stayed there with his brother Richard, who had been made King of the Romans (or Germany or Allemaine) by the Pope. Prince Edward, who as the 25-year-old son of the King was already a distinguished man at arms, stayed at the castle with de Warenne and such other distinguished men at arms as William de Valence. With its double-mound defence and its spectacularly perched keep reinforced with two projecting towers, Lewes Castle was indeed a mighty stronghold, and the idea of its being stormed by the raw, ill-equipped amateurs at Simon's disposal must have seemed laughable to the dashing warriors inside it. The royal army may have numbered 10,000 horse and foot, most of them encamped in tents just outside the town walls. They are believed to have arrived on May 11 (1264).

Simon led his troops out of London on May 6. He is said by the chronicler Brune to have had 'sixty thousand of London armed men full stout' but as its total population was barely 40,000, 6,000 might be nearer the mark, armed with nothing much to supplement their ardour except for axes, bill-hooks, and staves. No doubt more started on the journey than arrived. However, they formed only part of the force, the majority consisting of the knights, serfs, and mercenaries of the barons. Even so, all experts are agreed that the King's army was the superior in numbers and to a greater degree in equipment.

Forewarned of the King's movements, Simon halted at the village of Fletching (4323), 8 miles due north of Lewes and about 35 miles due south of London. This would have been in a clearing in the fast thinning Andredsweald, and it had for thirty years had a stone church, where Simon and his friends said their prayers. Among them were the Bishops of London and Worcester, Richard de Sandwich and Walter de Cantelupe, and on May 13 they set off for Lewes in a last effort to persuade the King to come to terms. Although their proposals were far from unreasonable, they were lavished with insults and returned with letters of contemptuous rejection. Simon gave orders for a night move and dawn attack.

It was considered unsporting, as well as unorthodox, to take an enemy by surprise, but Simon knew well enough that he could have no chance in a conventional, straightforward, and sporting trial of strength, having learned plenty about warfare on the Continent. At the first glimmer of dawn (Wednesday, May 14) his troops climbed the steeps of Offham Hill and formed up along the plateau, with his right in the area of the now disused grandstand (393110). The royal troops had spent the night boozing, and only one sentry had been posted as look-out on Offham Hill. He woke up to find the enemy around him.

As can be observed, Lewes Castle looms large from Offham Hill, although 1½ miles distant. By what surely emerges as callous but brilliant planning, Simon gave this as the objective of his greenest and worst equipped 'battle' (as he termed it), the Londoners. He placed them on the left. In the centre he placed the battle of young Gilbert de Clare, and on the right a battle commanded jointly by two of his sons. It appears that he kept both these battles under the lee of the spur that descends south-eastwards to Lewes from the grandstand, and behind them he kept a fourth battle under his direct command in reserve, which was another unorthodox but inspired thing to do.

Having issued his orders, he led a prayer for victory, with his soldiers prostrated on the dewy turf of the down, each wearing a white cross on his back and breast. (It is not quite clear how the mounted troops joined in.) Organised prayer figured large in the life of everyone, but in the setting of that May morning, with the sun rising above the objective, even the most insensitive must have been touched beyond the point of mere routine. Hardly any of them can have had prior experience of battle.

The Londoners began their advance. They had been spotted from the castle's battlements and must have heard the trumpets shrill urgently. Knights in armour, on armoured-clad horses and with the elaborate visor and plumes of Prince Edward at their head, emerged from the Westgate (now extinct) and bore down upon them. They might have been tanks for all the Londoners could do about it. They were caught in the open and took to their heels as the huge blades swished above them and spiked maces fell on skulls with awful crunch. Edward's men could release in glorious killing all the contempt and loathing that had been crammed into them. They were too heavily encumbered with their own armour to do it at any great speed, and consequently there was always some poor wretch waiting to be caught up. Some four miles of chopping brought them to the edge of the Andredsweald, where the search for victims consumed more time and enforced greater dispersal.

The King and his brother Richard were slower to muster their men. It is likely that they brought them from the area of the Priory to about where the prison now stands (4010) and were here assaulted by the two other battles of the baronial army; the discovery of skeletons and the whole course of events make this a more likely site than that marked by crossed swords (396113) on the map. It seems that these two battles, with Simon's behind them in reserve, came in from the north-west behind the spur, thus being unobserved from the castle. The cavalry must have led and no doubt caught the King's troops in the clumsy process of deployment. Great slaughter was done, accompanied by widespread scattering. The most important immediate result was that Richard, King of the Romans, was seen to take shelter in a mill, presumably a watermill on the marshes by the Ouse. Here he was surrounded, taunted with shouts of 'Come down, thou wretched miller!' and forced out into the arms of a blacksmith who quickly fitted him out with fetters.

The King had been fighting a brave but losing battle, in which his horse had been killed beneath him. Simon's men were closing in from all sides, and the guardians of the castle sought to hold them back by firing incendiary arrows into the thatched roofs of the houses on the south side. This hurled the inhabitants into the fight, adding cries of panic to the shouts, groans, and screams echoing across the stricken field from the mouths of men and animals.

Prince Edward's men meanwhile were whooping with delight at the discovery of an enclosed litter bearing Simon's personal penant. Since he had broken a leg not long since it was natural to suppose that he was inside it, and for long the men yelled, 'Simon, thou devil, come out!' At length they ran their swords through it – and impaled three senior citizens of London who had remained loyal to the King and been brought along as hostages. There can be little doubt that this was a deliberate ruse, or indeed that the battle had gone exactly as foreseen by Simon, for the ruse depended on the flight and pursuit of the Londoners.

Prince Edward at length rallied his knights and brought them back to Lewes. They were too weary and disorganised to do anything to rectify the astounding scene around the castle, a scene of smoke and chaos dominated by swarms of men wearing the despised white cross. Simon somehow managed to make contact with the King and to notify him that his brother Richard was in his hands and would be killed if he (the King) did not surrender. The King did surrender, and so too in due course did Edward. The countryside was now littered far and wide with fugitives, many of whom had discarded their weapons and dress of war. Some escaped to France, via Pevensey or Hastings, among them de Warenne and de Valence. Some maintained a form of cohesion in their flight and were surrounded and hacked to death 6½ miles north-east of Lewes – such at any rate is the legend, and it is strong enough to have given the place of this fight to the death the lasting name of Terrible Down (4915). According to the Monk of Lewes the number of dead on the royalist side alone amounted to '2,700, or less', and since he played a prominent part in the sickening task of tending the wounded and burying the dead he was better placed to know than any far distant chronicler. This might be one quarter of the royalist side, and such a proportion would be in keeping with the mood of the contestants, enforcing a high ratio of dead and wounded.

Having extracted various undertakings from the King, Simon took him on a tour of Sussex and Kent, making show of his loyalty to him. Edward was meanwhile placed in Dover Castle. Subsequently transferred to Hereford, he escaped, and in August 1265 he gained revenge in a battle at Evesham, where Simon was slain. But the parliament that he had constrained the King to summon at Westminster lived on.

King Henry's return

Chapter 10

THE HUNDRED YEARS WAR

There were few periods in the 13th Century when the Cinque Ports were not raiding some part of the French coast. In 1293 their private war erupted into an open battle in the Channel, with the Cinque Ports fleet supplemented by ships from Ireland, the Netherlands, and England's one remaining province in (south-west) France, Gascony, and with the French aided by Flemish and Genoese. Fought off Saint Matthieu, the battle ended in a great victory for the Ports and the return of their ships laden with prizes. Inevitably reprisals followed, particularly in Gascony. The former Prince Edward had now been King for twenty years. Involved in war in Scotland and Wales, he had no wish to be at war with France, but could not avoid it.

In 1295 the French assembled an expedition, which was to await the signal from an English traitor to fall on the coast of Kent. Failing to receive the signal, the French sent a reconnaissance force to Hythe. This was beaten back after making a landing, presumably by men from Saltwood Castle. The French then turned on Dover and had much greater success. Without any reported interference from the Castle, they burned most of the town and destroyed so many ships that Dover had to hire replacements for their entire quota as the largest of the Cinque Ports. The French did not stay long.

Edward I retaliated in 1297 by taking an expedition to Sluys, which is north-east of Bruges and is now well inland. It was here that the Portsmen launched their disgraceful attack on the squadron from Yarmouth, as related in Chapter 8. Nothing much was achieved on land, and in March 1298 the expedition returned, enabling troops brought from London for the defence of the Kent coast to return. Peace was made with France, and the Ports reverted to privateering.

In 1337 England had a king who was both eager and able to wage war with France. Edward III claimed nothing less than the crown of France for himself, and he raised an army of a new style, consisting of merely a fifth of cavalry, supplied by the aristocracy, and four-fifths of paid yeomen soldiers of the Crown armed with the weapon that was to prove its devastating power, the long-bow. For three years a large force of such men, eager and confident, perhaps 15,000 all told, awaited the dispersal of the many French ships that dominated the Channel and launched destructive raids on Rye, Hastings, and ports further westward. In June 1340 Edward audaciously led his warships – which included reinforcements from London, outnumbering the Cinque Ports – against a far greater armada massed at Sluys and won a great victory, thanks largely to the deadly fire of his archers. This enabled the expedition to sail, and in August 1346 the archers turned a humiliating retreat into another great victory, that of Crecy.

A year later Calais fell as yield from this victory, and the Cinque Ports were rid of their worst source of reprisal. The war dragged on, and again the English were on the verge of defeat when the Black Prince struck back to devastating effect at Poitiers in 1355. The amazing result of this was the arrival at Sandwich, on May 4, 1356, of the Black Prince with King John of France as his captive. They made triumphal progress through Canterbury to the Tower of London, where the King was hospitably detained until released in 1360 under the terms of the Treaty of Brétigny.

The euphoria of victory was short-lived. England was grievously debilitated by the Black Death and exhausted by the strain of waging war. Even in 1359 Winchelsea, off which King Edward had himself won a naval battle in 1350, felt the harsh barb of the avenging power of France. Three thousand Frenchmen landed, forced an entry into the new town, burned the church and butchered people taking refuge inside it, and spent a further twenty-four hours in plundering the countryside. This was the start of a period of great torment for the inhabitants of the Sussex coast, to whom the multiple clanging of church bells frequently announced the approach of fearsome raiders, pastoral messages being confined by order to single peals. Winchelsea bore the brunt, but in 1377 both Rye and Hastings were entered and almost totally burned. It was Rye's fourth raid within eighty years, and as well as possessing a small but new fortress commanding the sea approach, the town had received six grants of murage since 1329, that of 1369 being a substantial one, to include crenellations because of recent attacks and 'the perils which may ensue if the town remains unenclosed'. Yet despite the sense of awareness and the defensible nature of the town, the walls were successfully breached in 1377 and great anguish inflicted.

The raid on Rye closely followed the death, in June 1377, of the old, abandoned, no longer victorious Edward III. There was a feeling of frustration in England, which was stirred towards violence by demobilised bowmen who had shot down knights on the battlefield and felt no subservience towards them at home. In 1381 it erupted in a great rising under a man of Maidstone, Wat Tyler. Beginning in Dartford, it spread to Rochester, where demands for the release of prisoners from the castle were speedily met, then to Maidstone, where the prison gates were thrown open, and then to Canterbury, where the rebels occupied the castle and had a rampage round the city, destroying many papers and much property of the ruling class. Defiance spread to other counties on either side of the Thames and culminated in a tremendous massing of the rebels on Blackheath.

From here they stormed into London quite unopposed, entered the Tower, and dragged Archbishop Sudbury of Canterbury and Treasurer Hales to execution by beheading on Tower Hill. After various other atrocities had been committed, Wat Tyler presented his demands to the 16-year-old King Richard II, who listened attentively. Then Tyler was suddenly struck down and killed, on the instigation of the Mayor. With brilliant presence of mind Richard called to the people, 'I will be your leader. You shall have from me all you seek. Only follow me to the fields outside.' They followed him, and from the nearby fields they in due course dispersed to their homes, giving the forces of the law the chance to rally and to exact retribution.

The fact of this rampage, by peasants armed with 'bills and bows', reveals the inadequacy of the arrangements for local defence. These consisted of an extension of the feudal system, under which every man was under an obligation to keep arms according to his social rank. Thus large property owners had their own men-at-arms, and smaller ones combined together to select, employ, and equip local men as their required quota of soldiers. Such quotas were to be named the trained bands, but they clearly lacked training or means of summons – probably both – at the time of Tyler's revolt.

Ironically, the trained bands that were to gain greatest fame were those raised by guilds of merchants of the City of London, and having received ample warning of his coming, the forerunners of these trained bands bore the greatest shame for Tyler's entry into the Tower. Furthermore the Londoners had special reason to take pride in military service, for under a charter granted them by Edward III in 1327 they were exempted from impressment and from serving abroad against their will. (It followed that no recruiting party could enter the City without royal warrant, which in turn accounts for the pride felt by those few regiments, or their descendants, who have been granted the privilege of marching through the City with drums beating, bayonets fixed, and colours flying, namely The Buffs, Royal Marines, Grenadier Guards, Royal Fusiliers, Coldstream Guards, and Royal Dragoons, in chronological order of being accorded it.)

Wat Tyler's descent on London came as a diversion from concern about the Thames defences, which included a newly inserted chain and flanking towers. They had been put there because the French had penetrated as far as Gravesend in 1377 and carried off many of its inhabitants, arousing fear and anger, which were partly alleviated by a private act of revenge at sea, wrought by the grocer merchant, John Philpot. In May 1385 the French showed that their ambitions had enormously grown in scale by greeting the expiry of a truce with large and palpable preparations for an invasion to be launched from Sluys. The King's Council decreed that all men between the ages of 16 and 60 be summoned to arms, some for static garrison duty, some for mobile duty by the coast. The improvement of walled defences received urgent grants of money and attention, to the effect at Canterbury described in Chapter 7. There was some jibbing at the demands made on people's pockets and property, as at Sandwich for the clearance of a passage for a defence bank and at Chichester for the removal of houses from the wall. But the penalties for disobedience were harsh enough to dissolve protest.

In the event the invasion never came. The first attempt was thrown out of gear by a demonstration launched from Gaunt, which had long been in alliance with England, and an even more ambitious project planned for 1386 fizzled out for obscure reasons, one of which may have been connected with the upset state of Charles VI of France's mind, another with the threat presented by the English garrison at Calais, and a third with the surprisingly energetic preparations made by the English to defend themselves.

A lull followed, until another King of England emerged with the will and means to conquer France. Having packed an expedition into small ships, Henry V sailed from Dover on August 11, 1415. He returned on November 16, preceded by the glorious news of Agincourt, at which the bowmen of Kent distinguished themselves. The people rushed into the water to meet the King and carried him ashore. He returned to France, won Caen, and returned to Dover with Charles VI's daughter Catherine as his bride and acknowledgement as his heir to the French throne. His next entry into Dover, again from France, was in November 1422. This time he was dead, aged only 34, and was attended by a cortege that measured 4 miles and had already been on the march for two months, with the monumental coffin surrounded by white-clad torch bearers and escorted by 500 men-at-arms with lances reversed, wearing black armour and on horses barbed black. Certainly the people of Dover were closely acquainted with the triumph and tragedy of Henry's reign. Yet they had reason to moderate their pride with a twinge of remorse, for by putting the Royal Navy on a better organised basis Henry accelerated the decline of the Cinque Ports.

Once again the English were unable to sustain the brilliance of the start to their campaign in France, and after humiliations at the hands of Joan of Arc the whole country sank into brooding and indiscipline, of which the worst example took place off the coast of Dover, where the company of the Navy's largest ship seized and cruelly murdered the Earl of Suffolk for his part in negotiating terms with France. Alleged fear of reprisals against innocent people and anger at 'the tyranny of the King's officers at Dover' sparked off a rebellion under a veteran officer of the war in France, Jack Cade. A man of Ashford, he gained a great following from men of property in the Weald and West Kent, and by means of summonses as for a national emergency he raised an army of several thousand and assembled it on that well sited springboard for a pounce on London, Blackheath, in June 1450. King Henry VI assembled some troops, on whose approach Cade withdrew some 18 miles, to Sevenoaks. He allowed the leading royal troops to come through the town and ambushed them at Solefields (now on the residential outskirts, about 530540). Their commander, Sir Humphrey Stafford, and twenty-four of his men were killed, and the shock of this blow, which presumably was delivered with the long-bow, seriously demoralised the whole of the royal force. The soft-minded King discharged his troops and fled to Kenilworth, leaving London to Cade.

However, the Londoners turned out to defend their city, and there was a fierce fight for the bridge, which began during the night of July 5 (1450) and was not won by Cade's men until late on the following morning, after many fluctuations and the burning of many houses. Among Cade's prisoners was his arch-enemy, Lord Saye, the King's Treasurer and Constable of Dover Castle, and he may have caught him at his home, Knole, Sevenoaks. He was given mock trial at Smithfield and put to death. But Cade could not gain the Tower of London, and the loyalty of his men began to evaporate when the King offered them a pardon. As they dispersed he took such staunch followers as remained to Rochester. But he had never had support from the Men of (East) Kent, and being denied the submission of Rochester Castle and that of Queenborough, he drifted into Sussex, where he still had a strong following, but not strong enough to evade pursuit by the Sheriff of Kent, Alexander Iden, who killed him at a place now named Cade Street (TQ 2060) east of Heathfield. Like Tyler's rebellion, this one began in spate and ended in flop.

In France disasters for English arms continued, following a breach of the existing truce that proved to be as unwise as dishonourable. By 1453 every foot-hold except Calais had been lost, and England was in no state to continue a war of which the title of Hundred Years is an understatement. Before it finally spluttered out, further retaliation was inflicted on a Cinque Ports town for all the savage raids they had themselves launched in their heyday. Sandwich was chosen as the objective, and in expectation of the event, of which milder precursors had been made in 1400 and 1438, the citizens had done more work on their defences than at any other period of their history. Its most impressive product, built in 1451, was a two-storeyed fort mounting cannon, placed at the south-east corner of the earthwork rampart, along which the Rope Walk runs today. This fort, of which only a few flints remain, was named the Bulwark. All entrances were now covered by stone gateways, connected by a stone wall on the harbour side and a palisaded earthwork round the land perimeter.

Early one Sunday morning in August 1457 4,000 Frenchmen arrived from Honfleur under Marshal de Breze. If standing instructions were obeyed, they would have been spotted by the watchman on perpetual duty, who would have sounded a horn called the Moot, at which every male over 14-years-old was to report to the Mayor at St Clement's Church. It appears that the arrangements worked, for the French had great difficulty in forcing an entry and suffered heavily in trying to storm the booming Bulwark, which controlled both the harbour and the southern approach. But they persisted and at length succeeded, and now there was stiff fighting among the flintstone, thatch-roofed houses of the town. Fires were started and rapidly spread, presenting the innocents with a choice often faced on the English and French coasts, that of being burned or butchered. The Mayor, John Drury, was killed, in memory of which a black gown has been worn by the Mayor ever since. Then in the late afternoon a relief column was seen approaching from Dover, and the French withdrew, their plunderous work not fully done.

As far as Kent is concerned, this fight would appear to be notable for a first and a last: it was the first time gunfire was heard in fear and anger, and more remarkably, and far beyond expectation at the time, it was the last time that a French raider gained foothold on the coast of Kent.

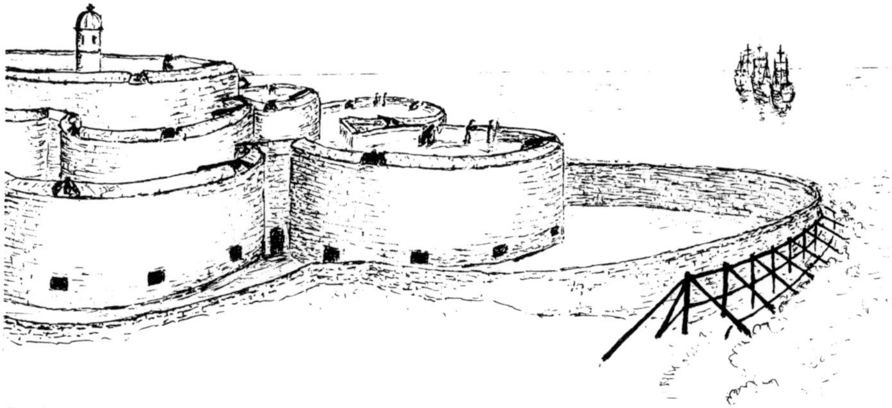

Deal

Chapter 11

UNDER TUDOR RULE

London and the South-East counties were spared the worst of the fury and horror of the War of the Roses. In the main they backed the winning side and supplied contingents to fight for the Duke of York, whose blood-soaked victory at Towton, Yorkshire, consolidated his claim to be King Edward IV. There was greater division of loyalty when the Earl of Warwick ejected his royal master, only to meet defeat and death in the real fog and confusion of the Battle of Barnet, fought in April 1471 only 12 miles north of London. This gained Edward a triumphal re-entry into his capital, and the Londoners greeted him with wholehearted fervour.

The people of Kent were more fickle in their loyalty, and when Warwick's admiral, Thomas Faulconbridge, sailed up the Swale with troops from Calais and landed near Sittingbourne, he was given ample support in his bid to restore the imprisoned Henry VI. Faulconbridge sailed on up the Thames to Southwark and was here joined by many men from Kent. An assault into the City from the east through Aldgate was at length contained and turned to rout by the Londoners. This led to the capture of Faulconbridge at Sandwich. He was executed, and so were many of his followers, at Canterbury, Rochester, and Blackheath.

In August 1485 Henry Tudor won the throne by his victory at Bosworth. Not until July 1495 did anyone seriously attempt to remove him from it, and this was Perkin Warbeck, claiming to be none other than Edward V (who had been incarcerated in the Tower by Richard III and supposedly murdered with his younger brother). Warbeck landed a motley of Austrian and Flemish troops near

Sandwich and made an attack on the town. It was triumphantly repulsed by the trained bands, and the invaders had to take to their boats, leaving 150 dead and alive in the hands of the locals. Henry VII was most grateful for this service by the unpredictable people of Kent.

The accession of Henry VIII brought about a continuation of Continental adventures, and in 1513 Dover and Sandwich acted as launching pad of another expedition. This gained great success in Flanders, with Austrian aid, but again the French showed their power to strike back across the Channel. In May 1514 they struck a new target on the Sussex coast, the town of Brighton, to which they did great damage. They also molested Dover, smiting some ships in the harbour while their crews were ashore.

In December 1538 Henry was excommunicated by the Pope. In place of the danger of raids, England was thus confronted with the combined Catholic powers of Europe, of which the mightiest was Spain. Henry had already given much attention to the building of ships, founding the yards of Deptford, Woolwich, and later Chatham, and it was from Woolwich in 1514 that there emerged the *Henri Grace a Dieu*, which at 1,500 tons and with a tremendous array of guns could dwarf and overpower any other ship in the world. None of the Cinque Ports could berth a ship even a quarter of this size, and they had to yield further prestige and importance to the deep-water ports further west, such as Portsmouth and Plymouth, which were also better placed to face the menace from Spain.

To protect the ships coastal defences were needed, and they could not be provided by the existing castles, which were not sited for seawards defence and had, with their tall and square keeps, been proved vulnerable to bombardment by cannon during the War of the Roses. Henry therefore turned his great store of energy into building fortresses of a new type, designed for seawards firing, using the money, and actual stone and mortar, obtained from the dissolution of the monasteries. He gave top priority to the protection of the anchorage off Deal, which was sheltered on the east side by the Goodwin Sands and was named the Downs, for the Channel could be controlled from here by warships too large to gain entry into Dover. Invading fleets had come along this roadstead since the time of Caesar, and in giving his personal attention to this sector Henry showed his awareness of its chiding vulnerability.

The 'great castle' at Deal was far removed from anything else yet seen in England and must have drawn many gasps of amazement. Still in prime condition, it is round and squat, oozing its pugnacity and thickness of hide, the forerunner of the pillbox. However, renovation work has distorted the pristine appearance seen by artists, by removing the gun embrasures from the lower bastions and replacing the higher ones with castellations of an earlier age. Forming three rings within a wide defence ditch, on which fire could be opened from many directions, the bastions would present even a modern attacker with a hideous problem of ever mounting complexity. The field of fire has in fact been improved by the removal of an addition, the governor's lodge, which was demolished by a German bomb in 1941.

The permanent garrison of this castle, as laid down in 1540, consisted of a captain, his deputy, a porter, and sixteen gunners (who drew sixpence a day). This would have needed substantial reinforcement in an emergency, partly to increase the complement of gunners, partly to provide infantry defence against ground attack, and it would have been supplied by the trained bands. It is not known how many guns were mounted, but there were probably at least a dozen, ranging in type from the cannon (which could fire a 60-lb shot 2,000 yards) to the culverin (17-lb shot 2,500 yards), the basilisk (15-lb shot 2,000 yards), the saker (5-lb shot 1,700 yards), the falcon (3-lb shot 1,500 yards), and other colourfully named varieties. The 32-pounder guns on display in the castle in fact date from the 18th Century but only small advance had been made in the two intervening centuries.

At a distance of just under 1½ miles and joined by a continuous earthwork, castles were built on either side of the one at Deal, of similar design but rather smaller. The northern one, Sandown, has been badly battered by the sea and reduced to a mere heap of stone. The southern one, Walmer, has lost some of its warlike character from being developed for the domestic use of the Lord Warden of the Cinque Ports – 'the most charming marine residence ever seen,' the Duke of Wellington described it. Like Deal, Walmer Castle is in the care of the Ministry of Environment.

Two other castles of similar style were built in the South-East. The one at Sandgate (TR 209353) was required so urgently that masons were imported from the West Country. Its siting here could indicate increased reliance on Folkestone harbour or appreciation of the importance of the high ground immediately behind, the future site of Shorncliffe Camp. Although its front has been battered by the sea, the remainder of this castle retains its shape but can be seen at present only from outside.

Camber Castle (9218) also stands forlorn, making lone display of its rugged but tattered might on a golfcourse. As can be seen on map on page 64, it commanded entrance up the huge estuary to Rye, but has since been separated from the shore by a mile of shingle. Although the estuary remained within the maximum range of its guns, they were dismantled in 1642, possibly for political as much as strategic reasons. The continual silting of the river had in any case eroded the importance of Rye, and it had long since destroyed that of Winchelsea.

Even as these new castles were being built realisation was beginning to dawn that gunners surrounded by stone – with ramparts around them but with nothing but the sky above them, preserving them from suffocation – were vulnerable to ricochets from shot landing behind them, and that a combination of earth and brickwork offered a better form of protection. It is probable that this new idea intruded in the gun emplacements named bulwarks constructed to cover the Thames at Gravesend, Milton, and Higham, none of which have survived. Bulwarks were also built at Dover, and although confused by later defensive developments, the earth and stone structure next the coast road above the Marine Station (about 316402) may well be the original remains of Henry's Archcliffe Fort. On the eastern side, with a field of fire in dead ground from the Castle, the Moat Bulwark was built at the foot of the cliff, and its remains can be seen on the left just before the traveller from inland enters the Marine Parade by the modern traffic circuit (where marked on map on page 16).

Despite alarms, the defences built by Henry were not put to the test during his life. In the years that followed internal affairs again gripped the nation, from which one important development was the appointment by Edward VI of Lord Lieutenants with responsibilities for defence. When the new Queen Mary announced her intention to marry the King of Spain, the owner of Allington Castle, Sir Thomas Wyatt, sought to dissuade her by the use of armed force. Volatile as ever, the people of Kent rushed to his support, 4,000 of them assembling at Rochester in response to his proclamation of January 25, 1554. They included a much diminished contingent from Tonbridge, who had encountered the loyal troops of Lord Abergavenny on Blacksole Field next Wrotham (6059) and been put to rout. However, when Wyatt began his march on London the opposition offered by Lords Abergavenny and Cobham, and from London by the Duke of Norfolk, swiftly crumbled, and once again the rebels from Kent entered Southwark and prepared to make an assault crossing of the Thames. They were equally true to precedent in their speed of dispersal. The mere determination of the Londoners, and their threat to bombard Southwark, diverted Wyatt to a flanking movement. The next bridge upriver was 12 miles away, at Kingston, where Saxon kings had been crowned. Wyatt found that he had first to repair it, and when at last he had crossed it and made progress as far as Ludgate, he had only twenty-four followers left. He gave himself up, to suffer execution. Many others were also put to death.

From the viewpoint of national defence, the only item of importance during Mary's reign was the loss of Calais, inflicted a year before her death in November 1558. This increased the vulnerability of England, and equally it increased the sense of insularity and defiance in which the people greeted the return of a Protestant to the throne, Queen Elizabeth. Her immediate concern was to build more coastal fortresses, and the need in Kent was for protection of the new naval dockyard at Chatham, to which oak could be transported down the Medway from the Andredsweald. A site was chosen at Upnor, 1½ miles down river from Chatham (757706 – DoE), and a riverside bastion of brick and ashlar was constructed here, with castle-style barrack immediately behind it. A fort was also built at the mouth of the Swale, on the Chatham side. Upnor Castle remains in good condition: the other has disappeared.

The human means of defence were quite as important to the Tudors as the fortresses, and no one did more than Henry VIII to encourage the citizen soldiers of London in particular. In 1537 he gave a charter to the Guild of St George, appointing its members 'Overseers of the Science of Artillery' (which included archery and musketry), and as such they provided the trained bands with many officers. Taking the title of Honourable Artillery Company, this corps was to survive every organisational change, providing units both of Artillery and Infantry in the Territorial Army, and it can claim to be the oldest in the British Army.

In 1539, as gesture of defiance following the Reformation, the trained bands of London marched at a strength of 15,000 from Mile End to Westminster, all dressed in white, except for the officers, who wore their private suits of armour. The people were thrilled by this massive display of might, pomp, and colour.

The trained bands were again called to arms when the private support given by Englishmen to the revolt in the Netherlands incited the wrath of Spain. Three thousand Londoners were selected in March 1572 for thrice-a-week training and armed with pikes, muskets-with-aiming-sticks, or the lighter firearms known as calivers. The climax came on May 1, when they were reviewed by Queen Elizabeth outside her palace at Greenwich and displayed 'their many warlike feats', undeterred by frequent cloudbursts. A certain Captain Thomas Morgan took advantage of the occasion to raise a privately commissioned company to go to the aid of the people of Flushing in their revolt against the Spaniards. It was from this nucleus that the corps evolved that in due course took the title of The Buffs and was eventually assigned to East Kent.

The tension rose in 1585 when Elizabeth openly sent aid to the Dutch. Among the arrangements made to meet an invasion was a warning system, which relied on a clear sky and a chain of beacons, each contained in an iron basket on a pole. In some cases they were as much as 15 miles apart, as had been announced to any potential foe in a history of Kent written by William Lambarde, which contained a diagram showing the two networks connecting London with the Kent and Sussex coasts. At times of alert every beacon had to be manned day and night by a pair of men. They were lit at least once on false evidence.

Word that the Spaniards were at last really coming reached Plymouth on Friday, July 19, 1588. It took ten days for the trained bands to reach action stations. The Londoners, perhaps 11,000 strong, concentrated at Tilbury, whence they were to make a hazardous crossing of the Thames, if necessary, by a hastily conceived bridge of boats, and with little prospect of protection from the coastal guns around Gravesend, which Lord Leicester found to be sited 'to the least purpose I ever saw'. Midlanders, at an intended strength of 22,000, meanwhile marched to London to form a reserve at Stratford-at-Bow. Under planning figures, which almost certainly exceeded reality, Kent and Sussex should each have provided 4,000 men for coastal defence and a further 2,000 for the Queen's main army. In addition each had its own mobile force, which in the case of Kent was placed at 13,000 foot and 1,000 horse and divided between Shorncliffe and the Barham Downs, both within easy riding distance of the command centre in the great house owned by the Queen, Westenhanger (121373). Each town should have been left with its quota of trained defenders, whose duties included herding the cattle inland and destroying outlying crops. But the duty for which there were most volunteers was to act as look-out on the coast.

The main English fleet engaged the enemy from the Western ports, gaining advantage because Henry's policy of building giant warships had been reversed in favour of more handy craft. Lord Henry Seymour meanwhile waited in the Downs with a fleet reduced by hard usage to twenty ships, which included a meagre contribution of seven from the Cinque Ports, only two of them being over 100 tons and none claiming status as a man-of-war. On July 28 the battle reached the Straits of Dover and Seymour joined up with the main, hard-fought fleet of Lord Howard. That night he despatched eight fireships that rammed the Spaniards at anchor off Calais and caused great chaos. Next day further damage was inflicted by gunfire as the Spaniards lurked off Gravelines, hoping to embark an invasion force. The sound of battle could be heard on the Kent coast, but the sight of the sailors put ashore at Margate and Dover brought no joy, since they were in a desperately debilitated state. Indeed, many died in the streets for lack of food and attention, and there was a great crisis of supply, to ease which Leicester himself hurried to Dover from Tilbury. Then the ships put to sea again, and it was a long time before the people of the South-East can have realised that storm in the North Sea had completed the destruction begun by the fireships and the guns. The trained bands stood down on August 19, probably feeling anticlimax.

There were seven more calls to arms before the 16th Century ended with the death of King Philip of Spain. He had aimed to follow Caesar's route into England (though not in person), but his troops were deprived by nautical forces from testing the efficacy of the first coastal defences erected by an English king.

Arundel

Chapter 12

THE GREAT CIVIL WAR

Just as had happened when Simon de Montfort challenged the King's right to wield absolute power, London again provided the driving force that pushed the conflict between King and Parliament from words to arms in 1642. By his attempt to arrest five Members of the Commons in January of that year Charles I aroused the wrath of every Londoner: the trained bands leapt to arms to give protection to the five and the mob raised such fury that the King fled northwards, escorted by his little band of Cavaliers. This virtually made war inevitable, but neither side had the immediate means of waging it, and a period of preparation and indoctrination followed. The people in the main were perplexed. Unless a zealot for the rights of King or Parliament, for high church or low, each was open to persuasion one way or the other, and there was consequently no clear-cut division of loyalty binding classes or even families.

One of Parliament's greatest assets stemmed from the failure of the Stuart kings to sustain the pride, pay, food, or equipment of the Royal Navy, despite the levying of the hated ship-money from inland counties. There had been war with Spain and war with France, bringing humiliations at sea, and after Charles had made peace the Spaniards and Dutch had fought a battle in the Downs, under the nose of Deal Castle, and put shot and men ashore without hindrance from the neglected defences. The Navy therefore were willing to follow the lead of London and give full support to Parliament, under a popular admiral, the Earl of Warwick.

It was just as important for Parliament to gain the loyalty or submission of Kent, thus securing their communications with Europe. By their arrogant rejection of the Kentish Petition – which included a plea that 'our sea-forts may be repaired and our magazines renewed' – the Parliamentarians in effect opted for submission, and on the report of an impending Royalist rising they made what would appear to be the first offensive move of the war. It was entrusted to Colonel Edwyn Sandys and a force of Londoners. They arrived at Sevenoaks on Sunday, August 14, with the intent of arresting Sir John Sackville, of Knole, and made for the church. The townsmen turned out to bar their path but gave way to superior force, and Sackville was grabbed as he came out of church. Sandys then found and seized five wagon-loads of arms at Knole and allowed his men to ransack the house.

This was a great blow to the Royalist cause in Kent, and the Roundheads – called thus because of the close-cropped hair of London's apprentice-boy soldiers – swiftly followed it up, even before hostilities became general. Sandys set off again on August 19, this time with a comprehensive brief to disarm all malignants and to secure all fortresses and magazines in Kent, accompanied by the Member for Queenborough, Sir Michael Livesey, with 200 troopers and 300 clanking, heavily armoured dragoons. Their first objective was Kent's largest mansion, Cobham Hall (TQ 6868 and on map page 100), which was the home of the absent Duke of Richmond, cousin of the King. He had left orders that there was to be no resistance, and a further five wagon-loads of munitions fell into the Roundheads' hands without a fight.

Down at Dover a great gain was made for Parliament on the initiative of a young man named Dawkes. At 2 a.m. on August 21 he scaled the walls of the Castle with ten accomplices, fell upon the somnolent guard, and gained full occupation. A half-hearted attempt at recovery was made by the trained bands, but it was given up on the approach of a force of Parliamentarians from Canterbury. Dover was in no mood to die for a king who had allowed dominance of the Channel to pass to the rival ships of the Spanish and Dutch.

Thus Charles's most important castle fell to his foes on the day before he made what amounted to a declaration of war by hoisting his standard at Nottingham and calling all loyal subjects to his aid. This was on August 22, 1642.

Colonel Sandys was meanwhile continuing his conquest of Kent. He entered Rochester after a brief fight for the bridge, took the ships in the Medway, and captured Upnor Castle while its garrison were out harvesting. He secured the 'malignant town' (meaning Royalist-inclined) of Maidstone. He then made devious, plunderous route to Canterbury, entered the city unopposed, and took over the county magazine. His troops then entered the Cathedral and (by a contemporary account) 'giant-like began a fight with God Himself, overthrew the communion table, tore the velvet cloth from before it, defaced the goodly screen', and performed other outrages designed to display their hatred of the reforms introduced by their prisoner in the Tower, Archbishop Laud. They lit no immediate spark of defiance in the people. Kent had been crushed and overwhelmed before any but a very few realised that civil war had broken out.

The main armies did not collide until October (1642), when they clumsily and bloodily fought the drawn Battle of Edgehill. The Royalists found that the route to London was open, and early on Saturday, November 12, Prince Rupert caused great alarm and anger by advancing on Brentford when a parley was in progress. After a brief exchange of musketry he crossed the River Brent and entered the town, which was held by a regiment of Roundheads, with some guns, from behind hastily erected barricades. Rupert brought up some of his guns and some Welsh infantry, and in a grim fight of three hours they cleared the town and gave the fearsome Royalist cavalry the chance to pursue the remnant of defenders as far as Turnham Green, where two fresh Roundhead regiments deterred the Cavaliers from further pursuit that day. Parliament had lost a dozen guns and 500 prisoners, as well as many men put irrevocably to flight or killed by drowning in the Thames. Rupert's men spent the night in sacking Brentford, which the European soldiers among them regarded as their rightful treat.

Turnham Green is today in the western portion of Chiswick and is still marked by a small open space (TQ 204784), lying between two teeming roads. Hither every Londoner who could carry arms was summoned, whether a seasoned member of a trained band or a newly enlisted recruit. They were on the march all through the night, and early on the Sunday morning were shepherded into position astride Turnham Green and its adjacent hedges and ditches, interspersed with newly arrived troops of the Earl of Essex's field army. It was a great concentration, estimated at 24,000 men and far outnumbering the weary Royalist troops who emerged from smoking Brentford under King Charles in person. The mere sight of this great array, combined with a few rounds from the Roundhead ordnance, expelled the King's offensive intentions, and he opted for a withdrawal to winter quarters, covering Oxford. The jubilant trained bands of London would never again confront the enemy so near to home, but plenty of action was in store for them.

Within Surrey there was almost unanimous support for Parliament, although there was less unanimity about how the county militia as a whole should be employed. Kingston was abandoned under the shock of the Royalist success at Brentford, but Essex promptly took steps to regain it when the enemy shrank from the confrontation at Turnham Green. He built a bridge of boats over the Thames between Fulham and Putney and sent his troops across to the south bank. He thus hastened the Royalist retreat, out of Kingston, back to Reading.

There is a report of a clash in Surrey around this time, of which the exact date and location are unknown. It appears that Rupert sent a force along the south bank of the Thames before he had captured Brentford, maybe as a diversion from his main advance. Its men bumped the Parliamentary cavalry in a lane bordered by high hedges and drove them into retreat. However, trained bands from both Surrey and Berkshire were in support, and they stood firm until almost overwhelmed, whereupon the Royalists were themselves forced into retreat by a daring counter-attack launched round their flank. The Parliamentary pamphlet on this affair claims that ten 'Cavaliers of Quality' were killed and that 300 men and horses were taken. It puts the Parliamentary loss at 300 men, which is unlikely to be an exaggeration and indicates that it was indeed some affair.

Another raid into Surrey in mid-November gained the Royalists the prize of Farnham Castle, which was evacuated by the unmilitary poet who had been placed in command of it. It was not to remain long in Royalist possession.

The war made slow penetration through Sussex, as indeed did all things when rain had moistened the clay that formed the road surfaces, slowing even the strongest horse to a laboured walk. Support for Parliament predominated but was by no means universal, and in Chichester the trained bands occupied the lay part of the city on behalf of Parliament while a body of light horse, raised by the clergy, drilled for the King in the Cathedral precincts. On the night of November 15 (1642) there was a sudden influx of Royalist gentry, and next day the High Sheriff of Sussex, Sir Edward Ford, entered the city with some county trained bands and a troop of horse. He enforced the submission of the city trained bands without a fight.

Fortunately for Parliament an army was at hand commanded by a man who had given recent proof of his prowess by wresting first Portsmouth and then Winchester from the grasp of the King's men: Sir William Waller. The first essential was to secure his communications with Essex's London-based army by recapturing Farnham Castle. Waller achieved this on December 1 by skilful use of a petard, which was heaved along a covered approach to within a few yards of the castle entrance and demolished both the gate and the morale of the defenders with one discharge. He could now march on Chichester without distraction.

With impetuous disregard of this danger, Sir Edward Ford set off eastwards to subdue the whole county, coercing men to join him on threat of death. Diverted northwards from his intended objective, Lewes, he bumped a Roundhead force at Haywards Heath in early December, probably on the high ground around where the church now stands (331239), which was then a scrubby heath. Neither side had artillery. The battle lasted an hour, in the course of which the Roundheads received reinforcements and put the Royalist force to flight, inflicting losses alleged to have been as high as 200. The majority no doubt were suffered by the wretched conscripts, who can have had no ambition except survival. Ford appears to have retained some control over his loyal troops, for he brought most of them back to Chichester.

Waller entered Sussex by the coast route from Havant. Appreciating the importance of Arundel (which Ford had not) he detached a mounted force to seize it as a preliminary to the siege of Chichester. The Earl of Arundel had accompanied the Princess Mary to the Netherlands and was never to return. The castle was held for him by a hundred men, and they were completely surprised by Waller's task force, of whom thirty-six made the assault while the remainder held the people of the town in check. Again a (or the) petard was heaved to within range of the castle gate. Rushing in on its disruption, the assault group grabbed the entire garrison without loss.

Waller arrived before Chichester (by his own account) on December 21, his force swollen to some 6,000 by junction with the troops of the staunchest Parliamentarian in Sussex, Colonel Herbert Morley, of Glynde, and with Livesey's regiment of horse from Kent. He first occupied the high ground immediately north of the city, the Broyle, and from here threw back a Royalist sortie. He spent the next two days investing the city and mounting batteries on all sides, with some interference from enemy guns. He put guns on the almshouses built by his ardent ally Cawley – which stands on the east side of Broyle Road on the premises of the Hospital Board – within 100 yards of the North Gate, and at even closer distance to the East Gate a gun was hoisted onto St Pancras Church (which has since been rebuilt). Shot was soon falling around Market Cross, after deflections to rectify overshooting. The defenders retaliated by setting fire to the suburbs on both east and west sides, and this drove the besiegers back, at the cost of great private loss and suffering and the demolition for ever of a thriving needle industry.

At 10 p.m. on the sixth day of the siege the Royalists at last made request for a parley, just as Waller was about to launch an attack from east, west, and south, in the last instance by blasting the Deanery door in the Roman wall by petard. He offered 'quarter and honourable usage', and although this at first drew an indignant refusal, the Royalists notified acceptance at 7 a.m. on the eighth day, just before zero hour for the assault. Certainly the Cathedral was denied honourable usage, and although the prisoners were in due course released they were deprived of their property.

The Royalist plan for 1643 was to make a converging advance on London with three forces, one from the North, one from Oxford under the King himself, and the third from the West under Waller's private friend and public enemy, Sir Ralph Hopton, who was to march through Sussex and Kent. By June elements of the King's force were falsely reported to have penetrated as far as Guildford, sending bleeps of hope to friends in Kent. This coincided with the issue of an order by Parliament requiring everyone to sign a covenant of support, under supervision by the clergy. Anger flared, with that sudden combustion peculiar to Kent, and led by gentry of both warm and tepid loyalty to the Royalist cause, the people rose in revolt.

Its main centre was a town on the road to Guildford, Sevenoaks, around which a motley of 4,000 armed men gathered, including most of the local trained bands. Aylesford and Faversham were also made rallying points. The County Committee meanwhile listened sympathetically to the demands of the leaders. This in itself drained the ardour of many of the rebels, and after further draining by two days of constant rain, barely 600 remained to confront the regiment of Roundheads that arrived at Sevenoaks, from London, on Sunday, July 23. Rather than fight them among the wooded hills behind Sevenoaks, the rebels withdrew towards Tonbridge, broke down the bridge over the swollen Hilden Brook (585474), and stood at bay behind it, sending summons for help from Aylesford by relayed pealing of church bells.

Colonel Richard Browne's regiment had arrived at Sevenoaks, while Livesey's marched on Aylesford. By Browne's account the broken Hilden bridge was carried by 'a most gallant charge by such gentlemen as voluntarily came to accompany us' and breached by planks. He then formed his men into various groups and took the town of Tonbridge 'after three hours and a half very hot fight'. He reckoned his casualties to be five or six dead and thirty or forty wounded and states that twelve enemy dead were found in the town, to which realistic figure he added his belief of 'many more' lying in nearby hop-gardens or drowned in the Medway. The relief column from Aylesford had meanwhile been intercepted by Livesey's and Sir William Springate's troops and had taken refuge in Yalding (6950), 9 miles short of Tonbridge. A few rounds of shot put some of the rebels to immediate flight, and a ruse contrived by the hardened and well experienced Livesey completed the confusion of the remainder. Three hundred surrendered and were encaged in the church, and enough weapons for 600 were picked up in the village. The dispersal of the rebel group at Faversham, and of other lesser enclaves, was achieved just as speedily by the intervention of columns of seasoned and confident Roundheads. One day's fighting had brought the rebellion to a close.

However long it had lasted there was now no hope of aid from the main Royalist army, for Charles had been diverted by the need to take Gloucester. In this he was thwarted, and in the autumn his central army suffered further frustration at Newbury, where by staunch combination of pike and musket the trained bands of London became the first infantry to stand up to Rupert's horse.

As for Hopton, he spent most of the year in subduing Hampshire and could not begin his advance through Sussex until late November (1643). Coming from Petersfield, his leading regiment entered South Harting (7819) on the night of the 23rd, just ahead of a regiment of Roundhead dragoons, and in a remarkable sequence of surprise, ruse, counter-ruse, and stampede, and with little loss of life, the Roundheads were ejected. Frost now hardened the roads and enabled the Royalists to advance at a speed that astounded the Roundheads. The fortified mansions of Stansted (7610), Cowdray (9021), and Petworth (9721), swiftly fell, with a fight only at Stansted, and on December 6, with the High Sheriff, Sir Edward Ford, at their head, the Royalists entered Arundel and laid siege to the castle. Mere threats, delivered by Hopton in person, were sufficient to obtain the capitulation of the garrison holding this key feature on December 9. However, when the Royalists continued their thrust eastwards they found their route barred at Bramber Castle (1810), where Captain James Temple made good use of this inheritance from the Normans. An attempt to bypass the castle and seize Bramber bridge was also thwarted.

Most of Waller's troops were around Farnham, and although querulously homesick, they repulsed an attempt on the castle made in mid-November (1643) by part of the King's army as diversion from Hopton's advance. When the alarming news of Hopton's success reached Waller, he briskly aroused both Parliament and his men to the crisis. Urgent summonses went out to the trained bands of Sussex and of Kent too. Somewhat unwisely, Sevenoaks was made the assembly point of an expeditionary force from Kent, and at once mutiny broke out, not so much at the prospect of fighting for Parliament as of leaving Kent. It was quelled under the influence of two executions, and four regiments (including Livesey's) set out, under the pretext of being eligible for service in Sussex under an enacted Association of the South-Eastern Counties, in which Surrey and Hampshire were also included. Other Kentish troops dug an earthwork on the Surrey border in Squerryes Park (next Westerham), crumbling remnants of which still give testimony to this gesture of insularity.

In the event Hopton's progress was stifled by the same reluctance to serve away from home, in his case of West Countrymen. He could not continue his winter campaign and himself returned to Petersfield, leaving Ford at Arundel with around 1,500 men. Waller acted with speed and flair. He first launched an attack on Alton, south-westwards from Farnham, captured the town and 565 prisoners, mostly Irish, and under cover of this stunning blow made a lightning march southwards from Farnham along the still frozen roads. Setting out on the afternoon of December 17, he covered the 40-odd miles to Arundel by the evening of the 19th, regaining Cowdray and Petworth en route without a fight. Early next morning he launched an assault on the town from the north and south-west, swiftly carried such field works as had been dug, captured eighty prisoners, and chased the remaining defenders, horse and infantry, into the castle.

In the next few days the reinforcements summoned from Sussex and Kent brought Waller's strength to around 10,000. The only hope for the besieged garrison was relief by Hopton, but this evaporated when he found himself confronted by the bulk of Waller's army on North Marden Down (8016) 18 miles short of Arundel, on December 30. Hopton returned to Hampshire, leaving Waller to reduce Arundel Castle at leisure. Again artillery pieces were lugged to the top of places of devotion, onto the church tower on the west flank and the almshouse on the south-east, a former Monastery foundation.

The parish church of St Nicholas stands above the town at its northern edge, and it was only from here that direct fire could be brought to bear on the barbican gate, 250 yards away, over the town wall that was subsequently removed under Cromwell's policy of demolishing defences. Deplorable though the use of a church for such a purpose may be regarded, it must be rated a considerable achievement to have hauled a cannon, presumably by pulley, to the top of the tower and to have positioned it in the narrow space between the parapet wall and the square base of the spire. The bombardment, which left lasting mark on the barbican, was combined with the cutting of the water supply from the adjacent lake. They together brought forth a request for surrender terms on January 5, 1644. Waller offered life (but not freedom) and civil usage, and at 2 a.m. next morning the two Sir Edwards in command, Ford and Bishop, gave themselves up in compliance. After daylight their officers and men came out in submission, the latter in a pitifully feeble condition. They numbered over 1,000 and had horses, oxen, weapons, powder galore, but nothing to drink.

The war moved westwards out of Sussex, but from June 1644 Waller had to wage it without his four regiments from Kent, who could no longer resist the call of home. It became clear to Parliament that only by forming a national, professional army, unencumbered by bonds of local loyalty, could they win the war. The resultant New Model or Ironside Army duly gained them the victories required, with large financial contribution from the counties of the South-East but without blast of battle on their territory. Yet the victorious soldiers had many grievances, and in August 1647 their Commander-in-Chief, Sir Thomas Fairfax, marched with his men from his headquarters at Hounslow, took occupation of Westminster and the City, and presented his demands to Parliament. The King meanwhile had been taken to Hampton Court, where he was kept under no more than surveillance, while his role was debated. Angry rumblings from soldiers camped at Putney, demanding rights of their own, persuaded him to slip away to the Isle of Wight, where he was kept under house arrest, blatantly a prisoner. Embers of sympathy for him began to glow, under only mild fanning by partisan Royalists. The people were impoverished and oppressed by many irksome regulations. They were in a combustible mood.

Canterbury was the first to explode, in rage against the abolition of Christmas festivities. The people of this fortified city, still the largest in Kent, rose in revolt against the County Committee, flung open the gaol, seized the magazine, armed 1,000 men, and prepared for siege. However, early in January 1648, the County Committee assembled 3,000 men of their trained bands to invest the city, and after a lengthy exchange of letters the rebels capitulated. Defences were dismantled as civic punishment: the city gates were broken up and burned, a stretch of wall on the west side of the West Gate was demolished, presumably with the aid of explosive, and guns were mounted pointing inwards on the citizens.

After incarceration in Leeds Castle, the rebel leaders were brought to Canterbury for trial in early May (1648). The jury evaded responsibility with a verdict of *Ignoramus* – they did not know – and at this there was a great resurgence of defiance throughout the county, which took practical form in the raising of a petition to Parliament. It was claimed that every male adult signed it, numbering 27,373, and it was announced that all copies were to be brought to Rochester on May 29 and that every petitioner was then to assemble at Blackheath– rousing echoes of Tyler, Cade, and Wyatt – and march on Parliament. There was massed defection from the trained bands of the county, and apart from Dover, Leeds, and Queenborough, every castle of importance and almost every magazine fell into the hands of the petitioners, either by words of persuasion or force. Dover Castle was closely invested and peppered with shot by the troops of Sir Richard Hardres, who had gained the sea-defence forts of Dover. It was saved for Parliament by the enterprise of its governor, Captain Brafield, who stocked it with provisions bought privately at his own expense, and the tact of Hardres's kinsman, Sir Henry Heyman, who took it on himself to organise the defence and to keep

Hardres quiet with a stream of courteous letters. Further diversion came with news that made the whole of Dover 'drunk with joy': the crews of the ships in the Downs had cast off their commander in a pinnace and declared for Kent and the King.

Alas for Kent, there was great fervour for the cause but no clear-cut aim or leadership, and when the Royalists imposed a commander from outside the county in the jovial but far from dynamic Earl of Norwich, the movement began to crumble. This in turn gave Parliament the cause and incentive to strike. The Commander-in-Chief, Fairfax, took command in person. He concentrated his force at Blackheath on the day appointed for the assembly of the petitioners there, May 30, dispersing without a fight those few who did come. The petitioners had in fact been thrown into confusion by the intervention of the Cavalier element, and of the 7,000 armed rebels who had been expected to muster at Rochester, at least 3,000 had not turned up.

Fairfax had four regiments of horse and three of foot, with some extra companies, numbering an estimated 7,000 troops, all regulars of the Ironside Army. He detached a regiment of horse under Major Gibbon, to march via Tonbridge and the Weald to the relief of Dover. He brought his main body to Dartford and encamped nearby for the night of May 30/31, having secured the crossings of the Darent. Next morning he sent a mixed column under Major Husbands along the coastal road for Rochester, while himself taking the main body further inland through the choppy, wooded country to Meopham (6466 also map on page 100). Husbands encountered surprisingly stubborn resistance at Stone (5774), offered by sailors and apprentice-boys. His men killed twenty of them and captured another thirty before gaining passage through Gravesend. Husbands now learned that the Rochester bridge was strongly defended and that he was to join Fairfax at Meopham. The latter's scouts had spotted the Royalist army encamped on the sweeping hillside between Rochester and Maidstone, around Burham and the prehistoric remains of Kit's Coty, near which Norwich had his headquarters. Fairfax had decided on a right-flanking movement and sent his troops swarming down the steep slopes into the Medway valley and onwards to the heathland by East Malling (7057), where they encamped for the night, only 3½ miles from the bustling growing town of Maidstone. They had marched 20 miles through difficult country.

Norwich had ample news of their coming from terrified refugees and had been able to see the dust they put up. Next morning, June 1, he put two regiments in Maidstone and a further 1,000 men to cover the Aylesford crossing (7258), while waiting to see whether Fairfax intended to come northwards or eastwards before moving his main reserve. In the event he continued south-eastwards, using Oaken Wood for concealment and a demonstration of strength to keep attention fixed on the Aylesford bridge. He crossed the Medway by the Teston-Farleigh bridge (7053) and gained Loose (7552), where his men dispersed a few defenders and crossed the River Loose by its ford. A good view of Maidstone could be obtained from the high ground, little more than a mile away. Although his men

THE BATTLE OF MAIDSTONE

Published in 1719 with John Harris's 'History of Kent', this map gives a good impression of the country crossed by Fairfax's troops in their advance on Maidstone. Names of places mentioned in the text are underlined.

Scale
0 1 2 3 4 5 miles

had had another tiring day's march, and although he was himself suffering from gout, which obliged him to travel by coach, Fairfax decided to force an immediate entry into the town. He sent his dragoons up the hill towards it. The time, by his own reckoning, was 7 p.m.

At this hour a Royalist trooper galloped into the town with first news of the enemy's approach. Norwich had entrusted its defence to the best regiments he had, both commanded by local men, Sir William Brockman and Sir John Mayney, and they had built barricades and placed cannon at the main cross-roads. Brockman himself rode off to Aylesford and came back with 800 reinforcements, cavaliers, watermen, and London apprentices. No reinforcement arrived from the main army. Norwich held council of war, heard a wide variety of views expressed, and did nothing.

The Roundhead dragoons were fired upon from hedgerows and thrown into confusion. Fairfax rose to the crisis. He hobbled from his coach, waved aside protests from his aides, mounted a horse, and according to an eyewitness 'exposed himself to great danger', a towering, darkly armoured figure. His troops rallied and drove back the Royalists, who lost Brockman wounded in this sharp and decisive preliminary. Hewson's 8th Foot began the storming of the town as daylight faded at 9 p.m. and the dragoons completed the rout of Brockman's cavaliers. The Roundheads met tough resistance. They reported that every house was a fortress, that every street was 'got by inches', and that shot from eight pieces of cannot smote them 'above twenty times'. Yet by midnight the Royalists had been driven into St Faith's cemetery, on the far edge of the town, up a lane that has ever since had the name of Havock. By one they had surrendered, leaving the Roundheads to count a tally of 300 dead or wounded enemy, 1,400 prisoners, 500 horses, 3,000 arms, 8 cannon, 9 colours, 16 barrels of powder, and 12 tons of match.

The truth would appear to be that the Royalists initially fought with great bravery and devotion, hence their high casualties, but that they were quite unable to match the team work of the professional soldiers constantly coming at them with thud of musket butt and stab of pike, and with darkness accentuating the disparity in training there was a sudden collapse of morale and widespread surrender. An Army spokesman stated, in a letter to the Speaker, 'We have not lost above 40 at the utmost, amongst which no officer of quality, but the truly valiant and religious Captain Price.' A fair purchase.

Lord Norwich had, according to Fairfax's intelligence, 8,000 men uncommitted to this battle. News of its result brought about a swift reduction: about a third of the Kentish petitioners decided that they were urgently needed on their farms, and a number of Cavaliers set off for Sandwich and thence took ship for Holland in hope of obtaining reinforcements. Norwich withdrew on Rochester, tried but failed to seize the ships in the Medway, and then led such men as would follow northwards to link up with fellow Cavaliers in Essex, leaving Rochester bridge broken behind him. Of this party, 1,500 survived a most hazardous crossing of the Thames from Greenwich. They were eventually slain or captured at Colchester.

Major Gibbon and his horsemen made good progress through Tonbridge and the Weald, scattering various groups of amateur rebels, of which the one that briefly contested the Roundheads on the northern outskirts of Wye (TR 0546) laid the myth of a great battle. Gibbon joined forces with Colonel Rich's regiment, from the main army, and they together put the men besieging Dover Castle to hurried flight. Rich pursued them to Canterbury, where many fugitive soldiers from the west had also sought protection behind its punitively breached wall. Fairfax himself closed on them from Rochester, and by offering fair terms to local rebels, as opposed to professional Cavaliers, he swiftly obtained their surrender. Three thousand weapons were laid down in the Cathedral and its precincts. This was on June 9.

All that remained in Cavalier possession were the three castles built by Henry VIII for the protection of ships in the Downs, at Sandown, Deal, and Walmer. Their reduction was entrusted to Colonel Rich, with aid from Gibbon's and Sir Michael Livesey's regiments. Lacking artillery, he had to settle for a siege, and his means of laying it were reduced at the end of June by the despatch of Livesey with all available mounted troops to the Sevenoaks area. He was ordered there because Parliament had received warning of a further outbreak of Royalist risings.

This move proved timely. Arrived at Sevenoaks on the night of July 2, Livesey was ordered to Kingston-on-Thames on the 4th. A renegade Parliamentarian, the Earl of Peterborough, was planning a rising from this town with the young Duke of Buckingham. Led by some of Rich's horse, Livesey's troops routed a covering force with such despatch that they burst into Kingston without opposition and put the rebel leaders to flight, Peterborough northwards, to be taken at St Neots, Buckingham eastwards to refuge in Holland. Some of their adherents, said to be 600 mounted men, meanwhile took possession of Reigate. They left it on the approach of Livesey and were also driven northwards and to disintegration, although not until they had shown some spirit in a clash where Surbiton now stands and in another when retreating through Kingston. They caused sufficient alarm in Parliament for orders to be issued that Farnham Castle (which had spent a fortnight in Royalist hands in November 1642 and a day in January 1645), Reigate Castle, and Starborough Castle (which stood between Lingfield and Edenbridge) were to be rendered indefensible. Of these three inheritances from Norman and medieval times, Farnham alone escaped destruction.

Having freed Surrey from contamination – and when his troops subsequently returned there on garrison duty they behaved so outrageously that they were ordered back to Kent – Livesey marched into Sussex, where a widespread outbreak of defiance had erupted with the seizure of the magazine at Horsham. The mere arrival of his fearsome troopers at Horsham supplied the prick to burst the bubble, and he now received urgent summons to return to Walmer. It was a journey of 80 miles along dusty roads, and the indefatigable Livesey inspired such resolution in his men that they did it in two days.

The cause of the alarm was an attempt to relieve Walmer Castle, made by four ships from Holland on July 5, showing a rare degree of coordination of the

Royalist plans. The attempt was thwarted after a fierce fire fight at close quarters. A further attempt was made on the 9th, this time by men in fifteen pinnaces, and also beaten off. Dispirited, the sixty men holding Walmer Castle surrendered on the 12th, although still well stocked to continue the siege.

Deal and Sandown proved tougher nuts to crack, even though Rich now had two cannon and two demi-cannon. The Royalists showed early in August that they also had designs on the Tudor castle at Camber by making an attempt to seize Rye. This was resisted by the garrison, and with the arrival of Major Gibbon and his troopers the Royalist ambitions disintegrated in dust.

A number of attempts to relieve Deal and Sandown were organised by the Prince of Wales, who was said to have been seen ashore with a landing party, showing 'the darkness of his father's image'. He gained some success and there were some fierce clashes here and there, particularly in sorties from Sandown Castle, but reports of the employment of Dutch troops, which doubtless were exaggerated, drained away the last dregs of local support for his cause. The Roundheads tightened their grip. On August 14 Rich reported a great victory against 800 Royalists, of whom he claimed to have killed eighty and taken a hundred prisoner, at a loss of only seven men. Deal Castle fell on August 25, in view of Royalist ships; it had suffered damage requiring a repair bill of £500, and its garrison could long have continued the fight. Parliament's admiral, the Earl of Warwick, now at last succeeded in driving away the enemy ships, and on September 5 the siege of Sandown Castle, the Cavaliers' last stronghold, came to its inevitable end.

By their inept splutterings of revolt the King's friends had convinced his enemies that he must die. The axe fell on January 30, 1649, and the groan that it drew from the assembled Londoners should have made the men who ordered the execution realise that they had severed themselves from their best supporters. During the brooding that followed, the Royalists of the South-East made their one useful contribution to the cause. In mid-October 1651, six weeks after his march from Scotland had ended in defeat at Worcester, the former Prince of Wales, now secretly acclaimed 'the King, our Master', led a horse through Sussex disguised as the groom of Colonel Gunter of Racton. His destination was Shoreham, whence he took ship for France.

Upnor

Chapter 13

UP THE MEDWAY

Alone of wars in English history, the Civil War was followed by no disbandment of the victorious forces. From the Navy's point of view this was just reward for services rendered, and the sailors showed their appreciation by making provocative demonstrations against Spanish and Dutch ships in the Channel. In due course England waged war against recently liberated Holland. Dover was used as a victualling centre, and the first clash between Blake and Van Tromp took place off its white cliffs, on May 19, 1652. Outnumbered by forty-four sail to fifteen, Blake was saved only by the bad gunnery of the Dutch and the succour sent from Dover in the form of armed merchantmen, in the best tradition of the Cinque Ports.

There was now a general manning of defences, and when Van Tromp sailed into the Downs in July, opposed only by a small detachment of the English fleet, he was deterred by the guns of Deal Castle and an unfavourable wind. Subsequently Blake gained a victory at Kentish Knock, 20 miles off the North Foreland, against De Witt and De Ruyter, which brought an influx of prisoners into Dover. But Tromp returned, and in a fight from Dover to Dungeness on November 30 (1652) he decisively defeated Blake and proved it by putting raiders ashore on the Romney Marsh, whence they removed 200 cattle. For the next three months Tromp was master of the Channel, but he attempted no further landing on a coast defended by many veteran soldiers despatched from London. Blake returned to the fray, and Tromp was at length forced back to the defence of his own coastline, after making a defiant bombardment of the forts of Dover in May 1653. The war was ended in April 1654, and almost immediately

Cromwell's aggressive England made war with Spain. Its only military effect on the South-East was the reduction of that troublesome base of privateers, Dunkirk, which was later sold to France.

On May 25, 1660, King Charles II 'received his own again', being brought from The Hague to Dover by a man-of-war on which the name *Naseby* had been hastily exchanged for *Royal Charles*. Having had ample warning, a huge concourse came to meet him, many wearing refurbished suits of armour that had long lain at rust. The guns on the Castle, forts, and ships offshore barked out their welcome, and as he landed trumpet clarions rose above the huzzas of the multitude. Journeying to Canterbury, he was met on Barham Downs by richly attired troops of horse, come from many counties, and by Kentish trained bands. On the third day of welcome he inspected his ships at Chatham, and on the fourth he received stately homage from the flower of the Ironside cavalry, drawn up in splendid array on the commanding plateau above London and traditional place of welcome or dispute, Blackheath. On the fifth day it was the Londoners' turn, and they were even more fervent in their joy than in the rage with which they had driven out his father eighteen years previously. The renowned trained bands turned out in force to line the route.

The rejoicing over, Parliament turned to the task of disbanding the standing army and of curbing expenditure generally, and as an inevitable result of the dictator's demise England's defences slipped into their familiar peacetime process of decay. However, there was no complementary curb on mercantile aggression, and once again England slid into war with Holland. The fighting opened in June 1665 with a tremendous battle off Lowestoft, which the English won. A year later the Dutch gained revenge in the great Battle of the Four Days, which began off Ostend and ended in the mouth of the Thames. It was a victory for De Ruyter over the restorer of King Charles, the former General Monk, now Duke of Albermarle, and the sight of the 'miserably shattered' ships that took refuge in the Medway greatly disturbed the diarist Evelyn. In men the English loss was put at 5,000. The great plague, the fire of London, and the self-indulgent extravagances of the King himself accentuated the physical and financial problems of replacing them, and early in 1667 Charles sued for peace. Since the Dutch seemed willing enough to come to terms, having suffered severely themselves, the English decided to concentrate on land defences rather than refit the fleet.

The defences that mattered most were those at Sheerness, controlling the mouth of the Medway, for great reliance was placed on Chatham both as base and dockyard. But Sheerness was a swampy and unhealthy place, and although a large sum was voted for the purpose, only sixteen semi-serviceable guns were installed at the point, protected by a single company of regular foot (Royal Scots). On June 7 (1667) a Dutch fleet of over fifty warships appeared in the mouth of the Thames – or in naval parlance, at the Nore. De Ruyter was in command, and daring sailor though he was, he was unaware that Tilbury and Gravesend were devoid of defences, and he therefore forbore to make a direct assault on London, merely demonstrating east of Gravesend and landing a party on Canvey Island (on the Essex coast), which was rapidly ejected. Sheerness was reinforced by a company of trained bands and forty-four sailors. No ship turned out to dispute the Dutch possession of the Nore.

On the afternoon of June 10 Dutch warships bombarded the battery at Sheerness. They killed one of the gunners and quietened the remainder. A landing was then made nearby by a regiment of Dutchmen and English renegades, commanded by the Roundhead Colonel Delman. The loyal English and Scots infantry, being outnumbered, withdrew after an hour's fight, leaving the invaders in possession of the whole of Sheppey. Report of their coming shook the mainland with panic. Warned by the firing of beacons, people swarmed inland from Chatham, Rochester, even from London, blocking the routes of the trained bands directed to the scene of crisis from all over Kent and Essex.

On June 11 the Duke of Albermarle arrived at Chatham from London, having put all available ordnance in motion. He found the dockyard staff urgently engaged on the removal of their personal possessions; indeed guard boats were being used for this purpose instead of towing warships to safety. The chain, which had originally been intended to provide a barrier under the guns of Upnor Castle (757706, also on map on pages 14-15), had been placed much further downriver, astride Gillingham Reach (7969), because of the large number of ships needing protection. Albermarle sent guns to cover it. He also had two ships sunk on its seawards side and prepared others for sinking on the landward side.

The Dutch spent the whole of June 11 in slowly sounding their way forward, without interference from the Tudor fort at the mouth of the Swale or from anywhere else. At 10 a.m. on June 12 their leading ships bore down on the chain and swept it aside as if it were a cord, to the horror and dismay of all English spectators. Its moorings had probably been loosened by a landing party or by mutinous sailors, the latter of whom were roving the area brandishing unhonoured tickets for arrears of pay and were heard shouting their greetings to English deserters on Dutch ships. They could now jeer at the most humiliating spectacle of all. A pinnace manned by nine Dutchmen drew up to what should have been the pride of the Royal Navy, the unrigged *Royal Charles*. They boarded her, found her empty, struck her flag with a derisive trumpet clarion, and towed her away.

Still showing no haste, the Dutch ships came level with Upnor Castle on the 13th, almost 12 miles inside the Medway and 1½ miles short of Chatham docks. The guns let fly, both from the bastion at the castle's foot and from an adjacent battery newly dug-in. They did something for the deflated prestige of England, but inflicted no palpable damage of any consequence, nor did the castle receive any hurt, although the Dutch long played their guns on it. As for the gunners, Pepys records that 'they shot till they had hardly a gun left upon the carriages, so badly provided they were' – whether with equipment or ammunition he does not make quite clear. However, they appear to have dampened the ardour of the Dutch, for having despatched some fireships and caused some great blazes, they began to withdraw, leaving the dockyard itself undamaged. They destroyed three

80-gun men-of-war, which had been sunk on Albermarle's orders but had their upper structure well above water level; in one of them, *Royal Oak*, Captain Douglas showed unique devotion, perishing on board. Another, smaller man-of-war was also burned.

The Dutch removed themselves with the same contemptuous leisure. They remained in the Medway estuary until June 20, making another landing to gain supplies and to destroy everything of any value at Sheerness. They had to leave three ships behind, grounded on a sandbank, but they carried off *Royal Charles*, and as a culminating indignity she was to be turned into a brothel. They remained at the Nore for a further five weeks, shaming English observers but finding Gravesend and Tilbury now far too heavily defended for more than distant probing. At last the ignominy ended. The Dutch departed, and in under a week, on July 31, a peace treaty was signed at Breda.

England's pride had suffered its heaviest blow since the Conquest, at slight material loss. Both by their number and by their behaviour the troops who made the landing showed that the panic they spread was out of all proportion to their menace. The fact of the panic might stem from two other facts, namely that Denmark had entered the war on the side of Holland and that the last invaders to come up the Medway were Danes, who had made quite a habit of it. Although close on 700 years old, the legends they emplanted struck an indelible note of terror, and among people incapable of reading, legends had great durability. Atavistic fears drove the people inland.

Yet while the land from Chatham to London is reported to have been convulsed with scenes of flight, anger and resolution animated the coastal towns of East Kent, which were more familiar with the sight and sound of war. At Deal (according to an eyewitness) 'the common people and almost all other ran mad' in their rage against king and government, and all went to work to make the recently battered castles defensible; at Sandwich it was reported that 'the mayor and jurats have commanded all to rise and man the decayed turf walls about the town'; and at Dover guns were mounted on the pier heads 'and at all convenient places'.

The speed with which guns were provided shows how easily the catastrophe could have been averted. Woolwich affords a good example. Comment on the vulnerability of its docks had been made six months previously, but only when the Dutch appeared in the Thames was Prince Rupert directed to eradicate it. He brought no less than sixty guns into the town, while the inhabitants abandoned their houses with cries of 'We are betrayed!' They were sited along the riverbank on a barren stretch known from its rabbit occupants as the Warren (436793). Some three years later they had more than the docks to defend, for this site and the adjacent mansion of Tower Place were purchased to fill a need emphasised by the Medway humiliation, that of a central place for the production and storage of munitions. The 31 acres purchased in February 1670 included 'sugar-houses, warehouses, tenements, stables, smiths' forges and other storehouses', and from them the Warren grew into both fortress and factory, the first and for a hundred years the only Crown establishment to manufacture warlike stores. It was also the birthplace of the Royal Regiment of Artillery, formed in 1716 to replace the complicated and expensive procedure of raising specified artillery trains. In 1805 the unpretentious title of the Warren was exchanged for that of the Royal Arsenal.

As for coastal defences, Charles II commissioned his Chief Engineer and Surveyor General of the Ordnance, Sir Bernard de Gomme, who ironically was a Dutchman, to construct bastions of the latest earthwork type, with bricked revetments, to cover the Medway and other fruitful objectives. Little remains of the ones he built in place of Upnor (which, as had long been intended, was converted to a magazine) at Cockham Wood (776713), Gillingham (776701), and Sheerness. A battery position was also constructed jutting into the mud from the western wall of the Medway's mouth. It was replaced two hundred years later by the Grain Tower.

Adding shame to the humiliation of the Medway, Charles made a secret treaty with France and provoked the unfortunate Dutch into fighting yet another war, which began with a tremendous battle off the Suffolk coast in May 1672. The Dutch inflicted quite as heavy losses as they suffered, but having also to cope with a land invasion by the French, they were forced on the defensive. Kent's problems were therefore primarily administrative, such as the reception of prisoners and of sick and wounded, for whom the arrangements were hopelessly inadequate, despite the familiarity of the problem. The provision of drafts was another hoary problem, of which the captains of warships in the Downs were made vividly aware by threats of violent resistance to any press gang sent ashore, in defence of the ancient rights of the Cinque Ports. They were obliged to turn instead to the rounding up of deserters, and by the threat of heavy fines on those who harboured them, 1,500 were regained.

The accession of King James II brought a shift in emphasis of England's relationship with Holland. The threat now was of a Dutch invasion in support of a rising to remove the Catholic king. James assembled an army on Hounslow Heath (TQ 1274), numbering some twelve regiments of horse and fifteen of foot. It was intended to overawe the rebellious, but instead 'the camp presented the appearance of a vast fair', and Londoners had no better entertainment than to flock to Hounslow for a view of this gawdy array of soldiery and their jovial motley of camp followers, male and female. It must have been the largest concentration of troops ever made in England in so small an area, and by further increase throughout 1688 James's standing army rose to a strength comparable with Cromwell's, over 40,000 fighting men. The fleet meanwhile kept watch from the Downs and Kentish Knock. It was drawn northwards towards the end of October 1688, and by the time it returned Prince William of Orange and his Dutchmen had slipped through the Straits of Dover. They landed at Torbay, on the coast of Devon.

The events of the next five weeks led James to realise that he could no longer count on the loyalty of his army. He therefore ordered its disbandment on December 10, having despatched his Queen and infant son to Gravesend, whence they took ship for France. He himself left London at 3 a.m. on the 11th, dropped the Great Seal in the Thames, and by devious route reached Elmley Ferry on the River Swale. He boarded a hired customs vessel here and sailed to Shell Ness, on the Sheppey side of the Swale's eastern mouth, where the ship had to take in ballast. Here the party were seized by a gang of ruffians, who had recognised one of the King's companions as a Papist refugee, and taken to Faversham. London was now in chaos, with mobs ransacking foreign embassies and generally spreading panic, which gained great momentum from rumours of the coming, not of the Dutch, but of Papist Irish troops, some of whom were said to be marching from the west and others were reported to be aboard some ships that made a mysterious appearance at the Downs. The Council sent pleas to hasten the march of William.

Released by an embarrassed magistrate and urged on by his friends, James arrived back in London on Sunday, December 16, with an escort of horse guards sent by the Council. Having been cheered with great fervour through the streets of the City, he took up residence in Whitehall Palace, where the 80-year-old Earl of Craven prepared to defend him with a detachment of his Coldstream Guards.

At 10 p.m. next evening, December 17, as the King was undressing for bed, word arrived that three battalions of Dutch troops were advancing from Chelsea with orders to take over Whitehall Palace. Craven declared that he would rather be cut to pieces than admit them, but James, who had been informed that others of his Guards had declared for William, quietly persuaded him to withdraw with his men. Thus battle was averted, and James spent the remainder of the night with Dutchmen on guard outside. Soon after daybreak he began a journey by barge to Rochester, where he stayed at a house adjoining the river. At midnight, Saturday, December 22, he boarded a pinnace, and after transfer to a yacht further down the Medway he made a bleak, wind-lashed voyage to France.

There was a certain grim justice in his route of departure, for he had held the post of Lord High Admiral (as which he had fought most bravely at sea) when the Dutch came up the Medway, and now drably-clad Dutch soldiers were in conspicuous and undisputed occupation of London, guarding the person of his son-in-law and successor as king and depressing the people with this unexpected cost of his expulsion.

Chapter 14

THE MILITIA

The accession of William and Mary made lasting allies of the two navies that had pounded each other with such fury, and this much reduced the threat to England's south-east shore. It also made war with France inevitable, and the French were quick to show that the naval power of the Allies was by no means invincible. In a battle off Beachy Head in June 1690 the French Admiral Tourville gained a victory over both English and Dutch and faced England with the prospect of an invasion made the more perilous by the earlier diversion of troops to Flanders and Ireland. Two years elapsed before it emerged that the French were planning to invade on a gigantic scale, and by now the old defences had been raised from their peacetime decrepitude to a state of bristling gunpower that would have pleased Henry VIII: there were sixty-nine guns on the forts of Dover, twelve at Sandgate Castle, and sixty-five spread between the triplets of Deal, Sandown, and Walmer.

In May 1692 Admiral Russell and his Dutch allies caught Tourville's men-of-war off Cape La Hogue at an advantage of ninety-nine sail to forty-four. Not content with gaining full vengeance for Beachy Head in the fight at sea, they closed on Cherbourg and La Hogue harbours and reduced the invasion fleet to cinders, sending James's prospects of regaining his kingdom up in huge columns of smoke before his eyes.

This was a victory of lasting consequence, giving the English the freedom to wage war on the Continent with whatever combination of allies might be formed to challenge the land supremacy of France. Thus the War of the Spanish Succession (1702-12) scarcely ruffled the shores of England, apart from one brief scare in 1708. This was followed by the anodyne of a peace that was not broken against France until 1742, when the regulars went off to support a Queen's right to the Austrian succession, having paraded at Blackheath for inspection by their soldier king, George II. In 1744 there was a sudden alarm of a French invasion, and this brought the Dutch back to the Medway, in the form of troops come to defend Sheerness at the request of the British Government: a situation almost as humiliating as their arrival in 1667. A year later, the Young Pretender's advance into England from Scotland roused great fear of a supporting expedition, and there was a rush to man what remained of the coastal defences. So far had the trained bands lapsed into disuse that the King's deputy lieutenants in Kent were reduced to calling on the general public to assemble for duty with whatever arms they had. Fortunately for them, the French were in no position to mount an invasion.

The great scare of 1745 emphasised the urgent necessity for a complete overhaul of the militia system, which although revised soon after the Restoration still relied on the provision of armed men by owners of property, on a scale dependent on its value. Its inadequacy was aggravated by restrictions imposed since William's reign on the carrying of personal arms and was given further emphasis by the arrogant and brazen brigandage of thieves and smugglers, particularly when the regular troops were away at war. The most notorious of its practitioners was the Hawkhurst gang, which (according to one of its members) operated at a strength of thirty men and thirty-one horses, the odd horse carrying extra arms. They terrorised South Kent and East Sussex for at least four years, until in 1747 the people of Goudhurst (TQ 7237) formed themselves into their own self-styled Goudhurst Band of Militia. Seizing the initiative, they forced the gang to bay in Goudhurst, and there killed three of them, captured others, and dispersed the remainder. Seven were subsequently hung at Chichester, three at Tyburn, four at Newgate, and four more on Penenden Heath, near Maidstone.

Yet despite both the internal and external threat, war had again to be waged with France and much debate had to flow in Parliament before a Militia worthy of a capital M came into being under two Acts of 1757 and 1758. It was to be financed, clothed, and equipped by the central government and, when embodied, would be subject to the same pay, discipline, and command structure as the rest of the Army, and liable for service anywhere in Britain. Its men were to be chosen by ballot, serving for three years with regular attendance at drills.

Arms were issued to units (from the Tower) as soon as three-fifths of the establishment strength had been enrolled. The West Kent Militia achieved this distinction in November 1758, which gained them fourth place among the counties of England and led to their first embodiment in June 1759, when news arrived that the French were again planning an invasion, in the third year of the

Seven Years War. The Surrey Militia, who had long held title as such and had a proud tradition, were embodied in the following month, July 1759.

The East Kent, Middlesex, and Sussex Militia did not receive their first order to be embodied until March 1778, when France raised another scare of invasion by joining the American rebels in war with Britain. The total men found by the four counties during this war was 4,160, and during the Napoleonic wars it rose to a peak of 11,313, of whom a majority (as shown by a return in 1793) were termed substitutes, or in other words paupers who had taken the place of men drawn by ballot able to pay both the individual bribe and constitutional fine required to free themselves from their liability. The regiments served far from their homes in war, and some gained the accolade of Royal. Thus the final list ran: 1st, 2nd, and 3rd Royal Surrey Militia; West Kent, East Kent, and Kent Artillery; Royal Sussex and Royal Sussex Artillery; 1st Royal East Middlesex, 2nd or Edmonton Royal Rifle Regiment, 3rd or Royal Westminster, 4th Royal South, and 5th or Royal Elthorne Middlesex; the Queen's Own Light Infantry, the King's Own Light Infantry, and the Royal London Militia Regiment.

To supplement the Militia, Fencible regiments, either of foot, horse, or marines, were formed for full-time wartime service, and in 1799, in response to a surge of defiance against the menace of France, Parliament authorised the enrolling of 150 Volunteer companies, to be added to Militia regiments. These were the part-time soldiers, who were to blossom forth in war with ardour and their own idiosyncracies and subside in peace, until finally acquiring a permanent organisation and the momentum eventually to supplant the Militia, with change of title to Territorials.

The alarms that caused the arming of so many citizens sprang largely from the dispersal of Britain's Navy and Army in the global wars of 1756-63 and 1778-82. They also reinvigorated activity on defence works, and the most important of those instituted and advanced during these wars was that of the Chatham Lines, which were designed to protect the dockyards from land attack. The plans for this new type of British project had to be copied from their enemies, the French, and were still based on those evolved by Louis XIV's famous Chief Engineer, Vauban. They adopted the bastion system, of which there were many refinements covered by an esoteric vocabulary of French words. Bastions were projections from which guns could put down mutually supporting crossfire. They fired from emplacements built into an earthwork parapet, named a rampart. The guns had a walled ditch in front of them, which formed both an obstacle to the enemy and a means of switching reserves, and the infantry had their parapets just in front of the ditch. The kernels of the two initial forts of the Chatham Lines, Townsend and Amherst, were rectangular infantry redoubts, which provided their occupants with subterranean shell-proof or casemated accommodation. That of Amherst (762683) is still in existence and can be examined. The development of the lines paused with each peace and regained momentum with the next outbreak of war. They eventually formed a continuous zig-zag of bastions more than two miles long.

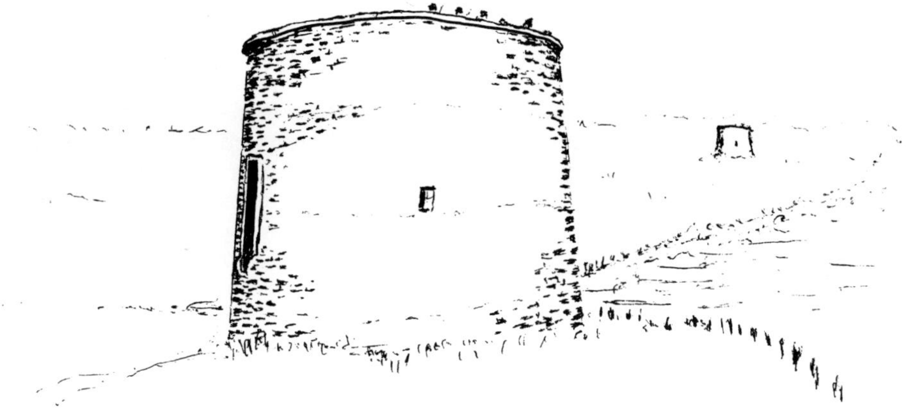

Chapter 15

WAITING FOR BONAPARTE

In January 1793 Britain embarked on a grimmer and more intense phase of war against the old enemy, who now rippled with all the aggressive vigour of Revolutionary France. The Militia were embodied even before the declaration of war, and later boroughs and individuals were authorised to raise their own units of Volunteers or Yeomanry. The outlook darkened in April 1795, when the British expeditionary force was ejected from the Continent, through Bremen, in a pitiful condition. In 1796 General Bonaparte crushed the might of Austria, and Britain was left as his only foe.

However, he could do no more than growl as long as the Royal Navy retained control over the Channel. The Portsmouth fleet made the major contribution, but the Nore fleet played an important subsidiary role from Chatham, and it therefore put the whole of Britain in peril when, in May 1797, mutiny broke out in the Nore fleet, in exasperation at a variety of grievances. Seizing the ships at Sheerness, the mutineers hoisted the red flag and blockaded the mouth of the Thames. The Government countered by ordering both Navy and Army to block their access to land, and among the troops who turned out for this duty were the Gravesend Volunteer Artillery, the North Fleet Volunteers, the Cobham Yeomanry, and the West Kent Yeomanry, straight from their work benches or farms. The mutineers showed that their defiance was waning by firing a salute on the King's birthday, June 4, with impressive ceremony and sufficient volume to disrupt some of the mortar on the Sheerness defences. On June 13 a party of soldiers boarded the flagship of the rebel leader, Richard Parker, and arrested him without opposition. It was the end of the mutiny. Parker was hanged at the yardarm of his ship.

By great fortune for Britain, Bonaparte chose this month of May 1797 to take an expedition to Egypt. However, by sending some troops to Ireland, in hope of exploiting a rebellion, the French kept Britain in a state of alarm. The Volunteers greatly expanded under a surge of patriotism, which was seen at its most exultant in August 1799, when the King held a review at Mote Park, just outside Maidstone. The 5,000 Volunteers on parade were drawn from forty-two towns and villages of Kent. They aroused great enthusiasm and had a great feast.

It so happened that Bonaparte sneaked back from Egypt during this same month, and in June 1800 he proved that his genius had not forsaken him by inflicting another devastating defeat on the Austrians. Britain again stood in isolation and peril and had to rely for salvation, first and foremost, on the Royal Navy.

In July 1801 a new naval command, superimposed on others, was entrusted to Vice-Admiral Nelson, who had just been made Viscount following his victory at Copenhagen that April. It stretched from Orfordness, in Suffolk, to Beachy Head, and he exercised it from Sheerness, where he hoisted his flag in the frigate *L'Unité*. As can still be observed in part, much had been done to improve the defences of Sheerness and to develop its harbour, which included two dry docks. Garrison Point had been turned into a triangular fortress by the digging of a canal in bastion line from the sea to the Medway's mouth. There were seven batteries all told, mounting forty-nine guns. Nelson showed no interest in them. In his famous words, 'The enemy's ports are our first line of defence,' and in place of merely keeping watch on these ports, as had effectively been done, he decided to launch attacks on them, much to the dismay of his Sea Fencibles. They resulted in heavy loss, in particular at Boulogne and Flushing, but they may have helped to diminish the French ambition. Peace was made at Amiens in March 1802, and Nelson turned to domestic pursuits, leaving Sheerness to recover equilibrium.

War was resumed in May 1803, with much depression on the British side after so brief and enjoyable taste of peace. This time Bonaparte brashly advertised his intention to achieve victory by the one method that could make it decisive, invasion. Having declared that he would dictate peace terms from London, he moved to Boulogne to supervise the assembly of a proclaimed 200,000 veterans of the Grand Army, being greeted by a salute of such volume that it could be heard on the English side of the Channel. Soon reports of the widespread construction of landing barges were also wafted across the channel.

Fortunately for the British a young major-general of distinction, John Moore, was already in the threatened area. He was given a brigade of five battalions, including his own 52nd Light Infantry and the first regiment to be raised and clothed as skirmishers and armed with the new Baker rifle, the 95th (later Rifle Brigade). His superior was a ranker popularly known as 'Old Pivot', General Sir

David Dundas, commanding the far spread Southern District, and the frontage he allotted Moore stretched from Deal to Dungeness. Rather than disperse his regular battalions along these 33 miles of coastline, Moore kept them on the seaside heights of Shorncliffe Camp (1935), which thus became and remained the most important station for field troops in the South-East. A statue of Moore stands inside it, as tribute to his skill at training troops. Mobility was its keystone.

The Government passed a Defence Act, renewing various regulations previously in force. They included a registration of all men willing to join in the defence of the country, but the response to this unimaginative edict was tepid, and in July a Levy en Masse was ordered, under which the King was empowered to order the training of males of all or certain categories and their embodiment if invasion seemed imminent, whereupon the Mayor of Folkestone assumed himself to be the King and ordered a muster of every man who possessed 'sword or gun or spade'. Authority was also given, in the event of invasion, for the evacuation of livestock and unwanted people, an operation known as driving the country which Moore strongly opposed, on the grounds that it would not be effective as a scorched earth policy and would merely cause panic and blockage of the roads. A scheme of greater value was the renovation of the beacon system, by use of semaphore and telescope. The target for the transition of a message from the coast to London was two minutes, through seven intervening stations.

In contrast with the impersonal approach of officialdom, appeals by individuals for the enlistment of Volunteers had great success. Not surprisingly the voice with the strongest appeal was that of the Lord Warden of the Cinque Ports, William Pitt, who happened to be out of office and could therefore live at Walmer Castle. By August he had brought the strength of the Cinque Ports Volunteers to 3,000 men, who were formed into three battalions and armed with a quota of muskets that must have fallen far below total. Certainly their appearance on parade drew its quota of mirth. In Sir Winston Churchill's words: 'Few things in English history are more remarkable than this picture of an ex-Prime Minister, riding his horse at the head of a motley company of yokels, drilling on the fields on the South Coast, while a bare twenty miles away across the Channel the Grand Army of Napoleon waited only for a fair wind and a clear passage.' The role Moore had in mind for them, as he explained to Pitt, was to make the enemy gape by their massed array on a hilltop, under the diversion of which he would attack with his regulars.

Neither the regulars nor the volunteers were able to reduce the people's fears of Bonaparte's coming. Moore sought to calm them by renting York Cottage, Sandgate, and installing his mother and sister there for a stay of two months. On the day of their departure, October 2, he rode to Dungeness, which he regarded as the most vulnerable and worst defended sector on his whole front and on which mark of his improvements can be seen in the battery position by road junction 089186. Here he received warning of an impending landing. He galloped his unfortunate horse back to Shorncliffe, noting that the Volunteers and Sea Fencibles were all turning out very cheerfully, and on arrival he found that it was due to a case of mistaken identity by the signal officer at Folkestone. The British preparations were in fact making better progress than Bonaparte's, and a few days later Moore received a reinforcement of three regiments.

Yet the British progress was far from even. To disrupt a landing on the low shelving beaches of the Romney Marsh, the Chief Engineer of the Southern District, Colonel Twiss, advocated the construction of towers of the type that had held up the British in a landing on the Bay of Mortella, Sicily, which name became corrupted to Martello. The Duke of York, as Commander-in-Chief of the British Army, backed the proposal, as a means of 'annoyance' to the enemy during his landing and of delay through his need to reduce the towers by artillery fire before he could disembark his stores. But the Duke could do no more than pass on his recommendation to the Master-General of Ordnance, which he did with commendable alacrity on August 25, and the resultant Committee of Engineers eventually drenched the 'entirely novel idea' in the cold water of a report not submitted until April 26, 1804. By now the matter had become a political issue, under the momentum of which Pitt was recalled to office in May. Although persuaded of the need, even he could make no faster progress than to convene a meeting of the Privy Council at Rochester on Sunday, October 21, as a result of which orders for the construction of five multiple Martello towers and eighty single ones, in Kent and Sussex, were issued to the Board of Ordnance on December 27. Work did not therefore begin until 1805, and by the end of that year only six towers had been built.

Eventually, two multiple and seventy-four single towers were completed, covering vulnerable stretches of coastline between Shorncliffe and Seaford. One of the multiple ones, with platforms for eleven guns, is on the seafront of Eastbourne (623997 – DC) and has been restored for public inspection, with other military exhibits. The other stands between Hythe and Dymchurch (129321 – MoD) with its rugged belligerence enhanced by additions made in 1940. Such single towers as survive can be seen as marked on Ordnance Survey maps. They are on display both at Dymchurch and Eastbourne with their complements of weapons. The one at Dymchurch was sited to protect the all-important sluice-gates and has one on either side at an inter-supporting distance of 300 yards; they were part of a stretch of six, the usual arrangement. It will be seen that the towers are elliptical, having thicker walls on the sea side than on the other. Most have a height of 33 feet, from foundations to parapet, and a diameter of 26 feet. The ground floor was used for storage and the first floor, entered by removable ladder through a doorway on the landward side, provided cramped living room for some twenty-four men, a separate officer's quarter, and a store. Their action station was on the roof, where they manned a 24-pounder gun and their muskets behind a curved parapet. The gun was mounted on a framework attached to the central pillar, round which it could be swivelled in any direction.

It must be remembered that these most conspicuous military relics of their day were not typical, that they had been rejected by appointed experts as being too vulnerable and that other soldiers objected to the dissipation of manpower they imposed – although no doubt they would have achieved their aim of causing the enemy great annoyance. Earth and turf formed the standard parapet, combining protection and concealment, and brick was used as revetment for gun pits. Unfortunately examples of such defence works are very rare because nearly all were altered or replaced by those designed to thwart the ambitions of a subsequent Emperor of France, Napoleon III, or of Germans. Indeed, the battery position by Dungeness (089186), which was one of four built there by order of Moore, would appear to be the best remaining example of a defence work of this period, and it is in peril of obliteration (in 1980) by modern development. It will be observed that its four 24-pounder guns would have been well sited to cover a beach that has since retreated beneath the advance of shingle.

A position that contains characterisistics of the anti-Napoleonic defences, although subsequently embellished, can be seen by the Coast Guard station at the entrance to Shoreham harbour (233044). The tackling rings, which formed the pulleys by which the guns were traversed, may have been part of the original equipment, and they were designed for the haulage of 42-pounder guns, one of which is reputed to have come into action when a single vessel made some distant attempt to stain the glitter of Brighton. The defences were thicker further eastwards. Newhaven, Seaford, Eastbourne, and Hastings had forty-seven guns between them, and Rye had thirteen, placed in front of the Ypres Tower in what was cosily called the Gun Garden. Forty-seven Martellos were built in the neighbourhood of these five towns, against twenty-seven (single ones) on the coast of Kent.

Dover Castle had no less than ninety-eight guns mounted in and around it, ranging from 12- to 32-pounders. Bastions were thrown out to north, east, and west, primarily earthworks with brick-covered approaches. The moat was greatly enlarged to provide the soil both for these projects and for the construction of ramparts on the inner side of the curtain wall, enabling the troops to fire over it. The towers of the Cannons Gate (nearest the cliff) were demolished in order to make room for a battery position, and other towers were filled with earth to form gun platforms, some with removal of their tops. The keep was strengthened and bore its share of guns. Prisoners of war occupied the dungeon. Whether or not they worked on the defences is uncertain.

An ambitious project for the fortification of the Western Heights, involving vast expenditure of bricks and mortar, was begun around 1780, soon after that of the Chatham Lines. It jerked forward after a slow beginning under the goad of Napoleon's threat, but remained incomplete until another Napoleon filled Queen Victoria's ministers with frenzied fear of invasion. Its story is best told as one, in the next chapter. As for coastal batteries, five were manned on either side of the harbour, today's harbour basin. The only positions that remain are those of Tudor origin, Archcliffe Fort and the Moat Bulwark.

The construction of the Royal Military Canal, which skirts 23 miles of marshland between Hythe and Winchelsea, was carried out at amazing speed when compared with that of the Martello Towers. It was proposed by an inspecting RE officer, Lt-Col John Brown, who found that the intended flooding of the

Romney Marsh might be a lengthy, as well as highly destructive, process and that the canal would shorten the line to be held and itself facilitate the movement of troops, while the enemy's progress over the dykes could be greatly hampered by demolitions. He delivered his report on September 19, 1804, and even by the 26th it had reached the Prime Minister, William Pitt, and received his approval. On October 24, assuming his mantle of Lord Warden, Pitt met land owners at Dymchurch and persuaded them that the canal would confer agricultural benefit, thus obtaining their agreement and eliminating the time required for compulsory purchase. Notices were sent far and wide for the engagement of labour, and the work began. Problems of employment and a dispute between Brown and the distinguished civil engineer, John Rennie, brought it almost to a halt, but Brown subsequently made good progress with the aid of military labour, and by July 20, 1806, the excavation was complete as far as the River Rother. The water could now be let in. It rose to a height of 9 feet and a width of 60 feet. It had nineteen wooden bridges which could be burned as soon as livestock had been evacuated across them.

Various refinements remained to be added, such as a road on the landward side and a parapet to conceal movement along it, and April 1809 had arrived before it could perform its full defensive and navigational task. By this time military interest in it had subsided to the academic, and the 180 guns that were to be positioned at jinks designed for enfilade fire remained in store.

The crisis in fact passed its zenith in mid-August 1805, when neither the Martellos nor the canal were in a state to offer much impediment. Beset by difficulties in harbouring his 2,340 barges and unable to ease the Royal Navy's stranglehold on his ports, the Emperor Napoleon (as he had made himself) accepted that the respite even of twelve hours, which he had ludicrously claimed to be sufficient for the release of his invasion force, was unobtainable. He turned his back on the Channel and let the world know that he had done so by falling upon the Austrians at Ulm, by the Danube. Nelson then emphasised the futility of a return to the Channel ports by his victory at Trafalgar.

100,604 infantrymen and 19,024 cavalrymen were by now engaged full-time on the defence of Britain, the great majority in the South-East. In Kent they were at their thickest in the great camp at Coxheath, south of Maidstone (7451), where the Duke of York held a review. In Sussex the records of Hastings, to which it was thought Napoleon might be drawn by the magnet of history, afford good illustration both of the expansion and of the fluctuation of the garrison troops. Until the renewal of the war in 1803 they consisted solely of Militia, ranging from as far afield as Worcestershire, Wiltshire, and Cumberland, with the one exception of the Lanark and Dumbarton Fencible Cavalry. By 1805 the garrison had grown from a single regiment to a brigade of five, one being regular cavalry, three regular foot, and the fifth militia. In February 1806 command of it passed to Major-General Sir Arthur Wellesley. He was soon required for more important duty elsewhere.

Nine years passed before he brought it to its conclusion, and three days before news of it reached England. Its bearer was a Major Percy, and he had been becalmed far out at sea in a sloop, from which he, the captain, and four seamen cast off in a gig and rowed for shore. They at last hit the beach of Broadstairs, next Ramsgate, at 3 p.m. on Wednesday, June 21, 1815. Percy and the captain procured a chaise and set off for London at a gallop, festooned by two French standards, which passed their message of victory to the people of Canterbury and Rochester. It had been gained by the former defender of Hastings, now the Duke of Wellington, at Waterloo on the previous Sunday, June 18.

Chapter 16

THE GREAT GIRDING

The dereliction of Britain's defences in due course followed the demise of Napoleon, accompanied by the suspension of all bodies of troops except the Regulars, who were much preoccupied with their Imperial responsibilities, and the Yeomanries, who were required for internal security duties. Through the somnolence of this era a call to action suddenly reached the 45th (Nottinghamshire) Regiment of Foot in their barracks at Canterbury, around midday on May 31, 1838. A Cornishman named Thom, who called himself Sir William Courtenay, Knight of Malta, had recently been released from the Kent County Lunatic Asylum and had aroused a fanatical following among some oppressed and simple yokels. Setting up his rampant lion standard at Bossenden Farm, Dunkirk (088597), he armed his men with clubs and drilled them, promising them the world and immunity from the weapons of their foes if they would faithfully follow him. A part-time constable – county police forces had yet to be formed – went to arrest him on this morning of May 31, accompanied by his brother. Courtenay shot the brother dead and put the constable to flight. Hence the summons to the military.

Since the summons came from magistrates at Faversham, the 45th did well to have a hundred men on parade by 1 p.m. Led by their commander, Major Armstrong, and four magistrates, they marched 4 miles towards Dunkirk, when they learned that Courtenay had taken his men into the wood to the north of Bossenden Farm. Armstrong divided his red-coats into two columns, to make convergent moves through the wood. After a long advance they came upon the rebels more or less simultaneously, finding them grouped in a clearing at a strength of about fifty. Mistaking the rampant lion standard for a white flag of surrender, one of the magistrates called out, 'You misguided and deluded men, are you coming to reason with us?' At this Courtenay called on his men to follow him. Lieutenant Bennett of the 45th advanced on him with sword raised and was in the act of striking when Courtenay shot him dead with a pistol he had apparently kept concealed. A cry went up from the troops; Armstrong ordered them to fire, having failed to obtain response from the nearest magistrate; the rebels charged with their clubs, and in Armstrong's words, 'I never saw men more furious or madly determined in the attack'. The 45th fought back with their bayonets. The fight lasted three minutes, and by the end of it eight of the rebels lay dead, including Courtenay, seven lay wounded, three others were prisoners, and the rest had run off. Apart from Bennett, a subaltern had been knocked down and badly bludgeoned, and a magistrate's assistant was dead, having been 'shot by accident by the military', according to the coroner's jury.

Bennett has a tablet to his memory in Canterbury Cathedral. At the moment of writing – April 1980 – he would appear to be the last soldier killed in a ground action on English soil. It was an extraordinary affair.

The institution of county police forces and the development of the railway reduced the need for units of the Regular Army to be dispersed around the towns of Britain, in the role of gendarmes, and opened projects for greater concentration. It was decided that Guildford, being on the line to Portsmouth, was ideally suited for such a purpose, but its inhabitants made it forcefully clear that they had no wish to be encumbered with a mass of regular troops, and a less populated and less cultivated area just inside Hampshire, that of Aldershot, was chosen instead.

Britain was aroused to her defensive needs by the sudden transformation of President Louis Bonaparte of France into Emperor Napoleon III. This was in 1852, and it brought about the reactivation of the Militia, now voluntarily recruited. However, instead of waging war against Britain the new Napoleon dragged her into alliance with him in the disastrous Crimean War. It was in the years that followed that he began to scare the British public, by his military adventures in Italy, by the belligerence of his press, and most of all by the production of an ironclad battleship, which could barge aside any British ship and, in British eyes, was clearly intended as the spearhead of an invasion. Lord Palmerston was returned to power in 1859, upon this strange tidal wave of popular alarm, and among his first actions was the appointment of a commission to consider the country's defensive needs. The soldiers and sailors thus appointed produced their report in February 1860, and after much debate and many changes of plan it produced one further layer of fortresses to grace the British coast. It is the largest layer, in many ways the most interesting, and the most derelict.

The forts had to mount, and provide protection against, rifled guns of high velocity, for as had been revealed in the Crimea, the technique of gunnery was making a great advance. New casemates were needed, faced with earth and providing overhead cover, yet open to the sky in rear, and behind them, standing no higher than the gun positions, a casemated barrack was required for the gunners and their infantry garrison. The heaviest expenditure was made on Portsmouth and ports further westwards. Eastwards from Portsmouth, the harbours of Littlehampton, Shoreham, and Newhaven were each provided with a fort. That of Shoreham (233044) was mentioned on page 117. Its gun emplacements may be of old Napoleonic origin, but its defence ditch provides an interesting example of a new development. The aim now was to lure the enemy into it, where death awaited him from the fire through loopholes in the wall of the ditch, or with even greater certainty from the projecting 'caponiers', which formerly had the function of protected passages but were now sited to provide devastating fields of fire along complete stretches of ditch, thus taking the attackers in enfilade. It was in fact an extension of the concept of moat defence available to the occupants of Tudor castles, and Shoreham Fort admirably demonstrates its potentiality. Only the casemated barracks, housing the combined gunner-infantry garrison, have been demolished.

Littlehampton Fort (028012) is on private land. That of Newhaven (449001) can be seen only from the outside because of the hazards involved in walking around it: a common enough fate for a fort of this era but one from which it may be rescued by the District Council as realisation of its historical interest grows. As can be judged from its massive ditch, it is far the largest of the Sussex three, which proves the importance the harbour had acquired. It was designed to mount forty-two guns and accommodate three hundred men, and it contains many additions and modifications to meet the demands of more modern warfare.

The most lavish expenditure in the South-East was on the protection of the Thames and Medway estuaries, although in many cases on emplacements for ancient muzzle-loaded pieces newly rifled. At Gravesend the New Tavern Fort (650747), on which guns had been mounted since Tudor times, was rebuilt to hold seven such guns of 9- and 12-inch calibre; recently restored to its last state of war usage, the fort is on display to the public as a pleasure-garden attraction and is being equipped with weapons of many vintages. Shornmead (692748 – MoD) contained more guns of smaller calibre, on foundations that sank ever deeper into the marsh; it remains derelict but impressive, impervious to explosions on the demolition range of which it is part. Cliffe Fort (707768) is on the premises of a factory but can be approached on foot. This mounted nine 11-inch guns, with an outpost of two 9-inchers in the position that can be seen upstream, and it also contained the first torpedo firing station, which was below the left of the casemates. This is the best example of a Victorian fort in the South-East, and although unkempt, its barrack combines a touch of elegance with solidity, in marked contrast with the drab control towers, which were superimposed in 1940 and emphasise the lasting utility of the fort. Further eastwards, the much smaller Slough Fort (835788), which is still visible as a wired and overgrown earthwork, guarded the one suitable place for a landing west of the Medway.

The Medway had acquired supreme importance because Chatham had embarked on the construction of ironclads. A fort of great strength and gunpower, which remained in service until liquidated by the Kent Oil Refinery in 1956, was built by Grain, just north of the Medway's mouth (890767). Exactly at its mouth, the circular Grain Tower, capable of mounting two guns, was installed in the mud and connected to the shore by half-a-mile of jetty; there it remains. Only half-a-mile further inside the mouth, a battery position, of which traces remain, was built immediately by the shore (893753). Opposite these installations, a mighty fort was built at Garrison Point, Sheerness, and it still displays its majesty and might as the home of the Medway Ports Authority. Further along the shore stand Albermarle Battery (909756) and No 1 Bastion (918753), successors of the guardians of Nelson's base, with a further outer canal line enlarging the triangular defended area as far as Barton's Point (940749). Stately forts were also built on the two Medway islands of Darnet (8070) and Hoo (7970), and there they continue to pay idle tribute to the style and industry of their Victorian builders (as can be observed from the southern riverside road) and to the fear inspired by the French ironclads.

The need for outer defences beyond the Chatham Lines was recognised during the wars against old Napoleon and has its mementoes in the remains of Fort Chatham (745679) and of Fort Clarence (738652). It was decided that the perimeter should be extended to the high ground to the south and east by the construction of seven forts, which was completed long after the fall of young Napoleon. Returned to private ownership after 1945, those of Borstal (733664) and Bridgewood (738652) overlook the Motorway, smothered by thicket. The outline of Horsted (752651) and of the two redoubts near the river, Woodlands (796681) and Grange (798686), can also be seen. Forts Luton (7667) and Darland (7866) have passed from public view, although remains may exist.

The importance of Dover was also in the ascendant. During the 1850s a great barrier against the advance of shingle was constructed, protecting the harbour from the west, and its name of Admiralty Pier presaged a resurrection of prestige as a naval base. The most important military requirement was to complete the fortification of the Western Heights, which had been begun around 1780 and been suspended after a second spasm of wartime activity had ended with Napoleon's defeat. As can be seen on map on pages 16-17, there were two main works, and the one on the spur overlooking the town was named the Drop Redoubt, possibly because of a legend that the Roman Bredenstone, which had been removed from it, had been dropped from heaven. The other, on the summit, formed the Citadel. There had already been colossal expenditure of bricks and labour on these two fortresses, most of it underground. It remained to link them with a further network of ditches, to construct caponiers of the latest type, craftily sited to ensure that there could be no escape from slaughter for any enemy caught inside any stretch of ditch, and to build extra accommodation both above ground and below.

The best impression of the size of the undertaking can be obtained from the Castle or the seafront with the view of the mighty gash that was carved through the hillside to provide a killing ditch running up to the turf-covered summit of the Drop Redoubt. Unfortunately, the complex of the redoubt itself can be viewed only in outline until its owner, the Department of Environment, makes it available for public inspection. On a ledge below it stand the foundations of barracks that housed a battalion until demolished during the 1950s. They were known as the Grand Shaft from the hole through the cliff that was drilled in 1802 in order to speed the movement of troops from town, to barracks, to redoubt, or vice versa. It contains three spiral staircases, each of 134 steps, and when peace returned to Dover, a notice appeared by one staircase (as vividly recollected by inhabitants): 'Officers and Ladies'. By another: 'Sergeants and Wives'. By the third: 'Soldiers and Women'. Recently renovated, the Grand Shaft is at times opened to the public.

Perched above the Grand Shaft, on the right side of the road of access from the harbour, the former South Military Road, is St Martin's Battery (318408), of which the covered emplacements last held 6-inch guns and the underground galleries pose an interesting conundrum of origin. The Citadel Battery (304403) also forms an intriguing blend of vintages, some possibly dating to the 18th Century. However, the Citadel itself has been converted to a borstal, greatly to the loss of students of fortification. It was probably the most elaborate fortress in the whole of Britain. It had barracks above ground, of which the officers' mess remains, for an infantry battalion and an artillery battery, and in its huge complex of subterranean galleries there was accommodation for quite as many again. It appears that the idea was to pack the strength to make a surprise swoop upon any invader who might advance inland after leaving a mere containing party to keep the Citadel quiet.

Through fear of an attack overland from the left flank, a fort was built, mainly underground, on the spur that descends upon the Castle from the north. It was named Burgoyne, and part of its overgrown earthworks and pillbox additions lie astride the Dover-Deal road. Access to the fort can be gained, with the commanding officer's permission, through the one barracks that still houses a battalion at Dover, Connaught. The main redoubt is heptagonal and has a caponier at every turn on the outer side of the deep and narrow walled ditch. The chimneys that sprout like mushrooms out of the turf drew smoke from the fires that warmed the soldiers in the casemated barracks, from the time of Victoria to that of George VI.

The most remarkable installation of the Victorian era was of two 16-inch guns, the largest the Royal Navy had, into a huge turret built on the tip of Admiralty Pier. The guns, which were of enormous weight, were placed in position after years of preparation in 1882, handed over to the Royal Artillery in

1886, and declared obsolete in 1902. They were greased and covered by boards, and there they remained until being discovered by chance and with amazement more than sixty years later.

One reason why the operational life of these guns was so brief is that the Admiralty Pier was extended as part of the great work carried out between 1895 and 1909 by which Dover was provided with its fully enclosed outer harbour and completed its rise in status to that of a naval base. It called for a further influx of guns. Two of 9.2-inch calibre were installed in the Citadel, four in the the new Langdon Battery (340424), overlooking the eastern harbour arm, and some of smaller calibre were mounted on the eastern curtain embankment of the Castle, in exploitation of the anti-Napoleonic positions. A further ambitious addition to the Castle, drilled in the 1860s, was a shaft enabling a battery position to be built in the face of the cliff. It bears the name the Shoulder of Mutton Battery and mounted 7-inch guns.

Another product of the alarms of 1859, roused by fear of the third Napoleon, was an outcry for the revival of the Volunteers, and in response to it the Queen issued a warrant, enabling boroughs to raise their individual corps. Their ranks were filled at speed under a great surge of patriotism, and when the corps were grouped into battalions over forty emerged within the South-East counties, the majority being formed within the metropolitan area of London, Middlesex, and Surrey. All were proud to name themselves Rifle Volunteers, which provides a reminder that the technological advance of the Army had been at the same turgid rate as that of the Navy, leaving some regular units to go to war in the Crimea still armed with the musket, the luckier ones having received an issue of French Minié rifles. The Volunteers cannot initially have had many rifles. Uniform was as chosen by each corps. Most opted for rifle green, but some favoured fawn or even a shade of mauve, and the Cinque Ports Battalion wore grey, with red facings and black braid, in deference to the Hastings Volunteers, who had remained in being as a rifle club rather than go into abeyance after the Napoleonic War.

Poets, artists, lawyers, shopkeepers, all joined the rush to enlist in the Volunteers. The units they formed were of a different social structure from those of the Militia, most of which were run on feudal lines under the command of a landowning grandee. Militia battalions were mustered for a month's training each year, nothing more. The Volunteers assembled briefly and frequently, usually at their own expense.

The catastrophic defeat of France by Prussia in 1870, and the abdication of Emperor Napoleon, brought little waning of enthusiasm for Volunteer soldiering, and indeed in 1871 it received fresh boost from an anonymous article that appeared in *Blackwood's Magazine* and was republished as a booklet. It was entitled *The Battle of Dorking* and foresaw just as catastrophic defeat for Britain, which shows that confidence in the Royal Navy remained lamentably low. It pointed to the vulnerability of the Dorking gap, as carved by the River Mole through the North Downs, and described its penetration by the enemy as the red coated regulars were in ponderous process of assembly. Having the sub-title

Reminiscences of a Volunteer, the article was not taken seriously by regular officers, until a distinguished veteran general, Sir Edward Hamley, brought such pressure to bear that in 1889 Lord Salisbury's Government authorised expenditure on the defences required. Sixteen forts were to be built and to be manned by the Volunteers, and since the men had to assemble at them, they were also called mobilisation centres. They formed a ring round London that followed the North Downs as far as Westerham (436563), then ran northwards along the Darent through Farningham (533669) into Essex via Tilbury. Gladstone's defeat of Salisbury then put the project into abeyance, and not until the latter's return in 1895 did the work begin in earnest. By 1908 sufficient confidence had been restored in the Royal Navy to persuade the Liberal Government that the forts were no longer needed, and the sites of most of them were resold to their original owners. It was a familiar pattern of swift expiry of purpose.

Of the forts covering the Dorking gap, nothing remains of Ashcombe (155511). Box Hill (177514) was the scene of the crucial, fictitious breach, and its fort was given emplacements for heavy guns, which appear never to have been mounted. It has slits for small arms through a thick concrete wall and certainly gives an impression of solidarity; part of its barrack accommodation has become the Fort Tea Rooms. Betchworth (201515) is accessible at the end of Fort Road, which was built by women convicts brought by horse and cart; part of it is privately occupied. Reigate Hill Fort (257521) exudes its pugnacity, a formidable bramble-encrusted structure behind railings and its deep killing ditch. Interspersed with these fortifications are those of the 1940 crop, which attained its most lavish growth in this region. The only fort still in Government possession is that of Halstead (near Sevenoaks, 499592), and its remains lie inside the Royal Armament Research and Development Establishment, which is no pretentious title. The public are not admitted.

As controversy raged over the Dorking gap, timely steps were taken to reorganise the Regular Infantry of the Line on a territorial basis. Although most regiments had been nominally affiliated to a county since 1782, they remained mere roaming bands until Gladstone's War Minister, Edward Cardwell, achieved his Localisation of the Forces Act of 1872, with far less opposition than to his abolition of purchase and reorganisation of the War Office. This brought the regimental depots to roost and allotted them permanent recruiting areas. Each was to serve two battalions, one at a home station, the other abroad, with the men interchangeable between them.

Regiments of seniority up to the 25th already had two battalions, and for them this move was unreservedly welcome. The others were linked in uneasy partnerships, and such was the dissatisfaction they aroused, particularly at the state of the home battalions sent to war in Zululand, that Disraeli's Government decided to bring the linking to an end. In the event his government was itself brought to an end by the Zulu War, and Gladstone thereupon appointed a War Minister, Hugh Childers, to bring Cardwell's measures to their logical conclusion. To the rage of the old and bold, he merged the regulars and the militia into large regiments, giving them county titles, with the revered old numbers consigned to brackets as mere mementoes. His Act took effect on July 1, 1881.

Seven county regiments thus blossomed forth in the South-East. The one already affiliated to East Kent was the 3rd or Buffs, whose ancestors had sailed from London in 1572 to fight for the freedom of Holland. As depot they had taken over barracks at Canterbury that were of Napoleonic war vintage, were overlooked by the Cathedral, and have since been sold and demolished. They took the East Kent Militia as 3rd Battalion and the title of The Buffs (East Kent Regiment), to which Royal was added within the brackets in 1935. At the time the title was made pointless by a regulation changing the facings colour of all non-Royal English regiments to white. Thirteen years of persistent protest brought about the restoration of buff.

The 50th (Queen's Own), the 97th (Earl of Ulster's), and the West Kent Light Infantry Militia became The Queen's Own (Royal West Kent Regiment), a title from which the brackets were removed in 1921, and in this union the Militia had the rare distinction of having their badge adopted, that of the White Horse of Kent. The depot was in old cavalry barracks on the northern outskirts of Maidstone, and like most barracks within range of Chatham, they were eventually occupied by Sappers.

The 35th (Royal Sussex), the 107th (Bengal Infantry), and the Royal Sussex Militia became The Royal Sussex Regiment, to the accompaniment of protest from a veteran of the 35th at 'the astounding impudence of a certain Mr Childers'. Their depot was just outside Chichester, on the northern side, in castellated barracks built by French prisoners of war, of which the keep still stands. Depot The Royal Military Police are their present occupants.

The 2nd or Queen's Royal Regiment of Foot had been raised on Putney Heath in 1661 in order to garrison the dowry that came to King Charles with his bride, Tangier. New barracks, which today house Depot The Women's Royal Army Corps, had been built for their depot at Stoughton, on the north-west side of Guildford. With the 2nd Royal Surrey Militia they took title that later became changed by switch of brackets to The Queen's Royal Regiment (West Surrey).

New barracks were also built at Kingston-on-Thames to house the combined depot of the 31st (Huntingdonshire), who had originated as marines, and a regiment to which the 31st had given birth, the 70th (Surrey). Taking the 1st and 3rd Royal Surrey Militia as 3rd and 4th Battalions, and an amalgam of the Militia badges, they became The East Surrey Regiment. Their depot barracks have since been converted to married quarters for officers of London District. The fort-style entrance keep has been preserved.

The 7th Royal Fusiliers added (City of London Regiment) to their title and three Militia battalions to their strength, the Royal Westminster, Royal London, and Royal South Middlesex. The 57th (West Middlesex) – the Diehards of Albuhera fame – and the 77th Duke of Cambridge's Own (East Middlesex) made junction with the Royal Elthorne and Royal East Middlesex Militias as The Duke of Cambridge's Own (Middlesex) Regiment, a title in which Middlesex advanced to main component in 1921. Initially, both Fusiliers and Middlesex had their depots at Woolwich, and both moved to Hounslow in 1895. Both then made further expansion to four regular battalions each, and in 1905 the Middlesex moved to a new haven at Mill Hill. In 1949 the Fusiliers were to return to the place of their birth in 1685, the Tower.

The Boer War gave Britain's citizen soldiers their first opportunity to go to war, and it was eagerly grasped. Almost every man of the Militia in the South-East volunteered to serve overseas, and their battalions either saw active service in South Africa or relieved regulars of Colonial commitments. The Volunteers raised composite companies to reinforce affiliated regular battalions, and in London the Lord Mayor raised a composite battalion, which was named the City Imperial Volunteers. They gained distinction on the battlefield and received a tremendous reception on their triumphant return to the City in November 1900. Many other returning warriors received as exuberant a welcome.

In 1908 yet another Liberal War Minister, R.B. Haldane, introduced important reforms, designed to make the Army better prepared for war. He converted the Militia into the Special Reserve, as which its battalions were to become reinforcement units, while retaining their status and seniority within their regiments. The Volunteers were reorganised as the Territorial Force and raised to a higher state of readiness, with the full integration – and consequent loss of individuality – of battalions into the county regiments. The combined strength of the South-East's seven thus rose to the massive total of forty-nine battalions, all relying on voluntary enlistment. There were eighteen regular battalions (Fusiliers and Middlesex each having four), eleven reserve, and twenty territorial, including six of the London Regiment, of which four were affiliated to the Fusiliers and two to the Queen's.

A further twenty territorial battalions retained their separate identity as part of the London Regiment, four being of the City and the remainder being County of London battalions; they bore such subsidiary names as the London Rifle Brigade, the Post Office Rifles, Queen Victoria's Rifles, The Rangers, London Scottish, Civil Service Rifles, London Irish Rifles, and the Artists Rifles. In addition, the Inns of Court formed an officer training corps, and the oldest corps of all, the Honourable Artillery Company, fielded an infantry battalion and two batteries of horse artillery. Then there were the City of London Yeomanry (Rough Riders) and the 1st (Duke of Cambridge's Hussars), 2nd (Westminster Dragoons), and the 3rd (Sharpshooters) County of London Yeomanry. Surrey, Sussex, West Kent, and East Kent also had their Yeomanry regiments, bringing the total within the South-East to eight.

As for regular recruits, it seems reasonable to suppose that the South-East counties provided a quota higher than average into the Royal Navy, through physical links with Greenwich, Chatham, and Dover, and through the tradition of the Cinque Ports; into the Royal Marines, through their depot at Deal; into the Cavalry, through the depots at Canterbury and Shorncliffe, which served all regiments serving overseas; into the Foot Guards, through the depot that in 1877 moved from Croydon into new barracks at Caterham, where from 1900 onwards it had to meet the demands of ten battalions; into the Royal Artillery and the Royal Engineers, through their depots at Woolwich and Chatham; and into the King's Royal Rifle Corps and the Rifle Brigade, whose links with London were cemented by the absorption of the remaining three Militia or Special Reserve battalions and who also had spiritual links with Shorncliffe and Dover.

An undoubted aid to the lure of a soldier's life, particularly in London, was the magnificence of the barracks – in the beholder's eye rather than in that of their stoic occupants – that housed the regulars. They had their forerunner in the guard house that in 1663 took more permanent form with the name of Horse Guards, next St James Park Gate, and between 1750 and 1760 was rebuilt in its present romantic Oriental style to house the Commander-in-Chief. The War Office was moved into Buckingham House, Pall Mall, in 1858, whither the C-in-C was forced to move in 1871, and it had a further move, into its great slab of Victorian grandeur, on the other side of Whitehall, in 1906. For the Sovereign's Household troops, the symmetrical and elegant Wellington Barracks, in Birdcage Walk, were completed in 1833 and, outwardly, still pay tribute to their team of architects. Chelsea Barracks showed less durability, being built in 1861 and rebuilt in their less elegant modern style in 1962. As for the cavalry barracks, named Hyde Park or Knightsbridge, they arose in their glaring red brick in 1880 and in 1970 were refashioned to the design of Sir Basil Spence.

At Greenwich, the Royal Naval College was established in 1873, taking over Wren's riverside masterpiece, which had been rebuilt to replace the derelict Tudor palace and converted, by order of William and Mary, into a hospital for naval pensioners. The opening of the Royal Naval College brought a well timed revival of naval influence to this area, for it closely followed the closing of the dockyards founded by Henry VIII, at Deptford and Woolwich.

However, the military establishments at Woolwich had greatly expanded. The Royal Arsenal had extended its domain by 3 miles further up the riverside, to provide space for the testing of ordnance; it has shrunk by now to barely half a mile, and all that can be seen of it is the massive wrought-iron gate (436792) erected in 1829 and a long, high, and dirty wall. The Royal Artillery moved from the Arsenal into some barracks that developed a superb facade, 1,000 feet long, (432784) overlooking the common, on which live rounds used to fall as a matter of routine training until the School of Artillery moved to Shoeburyness in 1858. The remarkable feature of the barracks, which must be the finest to look at in all England, is that they were built in two parts, in 1777 and 1802, without infringement of symmetry. Only the frontal section, including the famous RA Mess, remains, other parts having been replaced by new barracks, and all that remains of the old chapel, on the other side of the road, is the mosaic-adorned shell to which it was converted by a wartime bomb. The barracks continue to house both the Directorate and Depot of the Royal Artillery.

On the west side of the barracks stands Nash's Rotunda and its fascinating collection of guns and small arms, and to the south-east, on the opposite side of the main road, stands the picturesque Tudor-style building that was in fact built in 1805 to house the Royal Military Academy (or 'Shop'), which was instituted in 1741 inside the Arsenal. It was here that cadets were turned into officers of the more learned fighting arms. These barracks today house a few garrison troops and the RA Museum.

The Royal Military College, consisting of Senior and Junior Departments, was founded between 1799 and 1802. After occupying quarters at Marlow, it moved in 1812 into the stately buildings designed for it near the Berkshire village of Sandhurst, in grounds stretching as far as Camberley, Surrey. While the Junior Department flourished here, producing officers for the Cavalry and Infantry, the Senior ailed, until the Crimean War drew stark attention to the need for good staff officers. In 1858 it took title as Staff College, and in 1862 it moved into its own new building on the Camberley side of the Sandhurst grounds. This is an imposing specimen of Victorian architecture, making worthy complement to what became the RMC's Old Building when a new, far from elegant, block was completed in 1912 to house an ever expanding number of gentlemen cadets (as they were officially termed). There was to be further expansion in 1947, when the RMA forsook Woolwich to impose its title on Sandhurst as senior member of an amalgamation.

The Royal Engineers also originated at Woolwich, as an officer corps. In 1856 the Corps came into being in its present form by the amalgamation of the officer corps with the Sappers and Miners and established a training centre in Brompton Barracks, Chatham, which had been built in 1804 for troops manning the defence works. Standing above the dockyard and the naval barracks, Brompton and the adjacent Kitchener Barracks have remained a great stronghold of the Sappers, containing both the Depot and the Royal School of Military Engineering, increments of which have spread to other locations on either side of the Medway.

As for Chatham Dockyard, it had gained fame as the launcher of Nelson's *Victory*, and in 1863 it reached the zenith of its expansion and prestige with the launching of Britain's first ironclad battleship, *Achilles*. But the requirement now began to exceed its capacity, and it had to turn to building lesser ships and to repair work – a task of uncertain future. There are some fine buildings inside the Dockyard and the Naval Base, including the Queen Anne Medway House, whose occupant formerly held a full admiral's rank and status as C-in-C Nore Command and now holds only the rear admiral's appointment of Flag Officer Medway, although still with a widespread command. But to the casual visitor little more is visible of the dockyards than the huge and garishly painted figureheads of naval heroes of old, glaring down on the sentries at the gates. The Sappers retaliate with a statue of Kitchener mounted on a horse of great magnificence and one of Gordon, rescued from Khartoum, riding a camel.

Built in 1794, the barracks at Deal have since 1861 been occupied by the Royal Marines, who today have their Depot for juniors and School of Music there. The surviving block of the old barracks is a worthy neighbour of Deal Castle.

Hythe contained a famous Infantry establishment, the School of Musketry, occupying elegant barracks that had been built in 1809 for men of the Royal Staff Corps and Wagon Train operating the Military Canal. The School was opened there in 1853, bringing a wide variety of uniforms to Hythe, as worn by those attending courses. In the same year the first rifle was produced bearing the name of its place of manufacture, Enfield, at the northern extremity of Middlesex, by the River Lea. The factory here had been under Government ownership since 1812, and in 1854 it was decided greatly to enlarge it and to place it under the direct control of the Board of Ordnance. The manufacture of its most famous product, the Lee Enfield rifle, began in 1895. It was to remain in service, with certain modifications, until the 1960s.

The ranges at Hythe cover a large expanse of shingle amid the Martello towers along the coast, and it was here that the instructors showed how fifteen rounds a minute could be conjured with accuracy from the Lee Enfield rifle. The continual crackle of fire was a source of annoyance to some of the inhabitants, but it was to bring more than annoyance to the Germans in 1914. Renamed the Small Arms Wing of the School of Infantry, the school was moved to Warminster in 1969, and the barracks have been sold for conversion or demolition. But the ranges still vibrate with the smack of bullets, as indeed they have done since the days of Sir John Moore.

Vindictive's Return

Chapter 17

THE GREAT WAR

The outbreak of war on August 4, 1914, brought great activity to all the depots in the South-East and a rush to the coast, for defensive duties, by the territorials of the Home Counties Division. From Canterbury, Shorncliffe, and Dover, the 2nd Cavalry Brigade and the 10th and 12th Infantry Brigades set out to join the British Expeditionary Force, taking a circuitous route through Southampton. Newhaven alone made contribution, of the South-East's ports, to the BEF's despatch, being a conveyor of stores.

As the regular infantry left Dover by train, its people had the thrill of hearing and seeing combat aircraft. Four squadrons of the Royal Flying Corps flew from the field by the cliffs above the eastern harbour arm (337427), bound for Amiens, between August 13 and 15. It was the first time that flying machines had gone to war.

Sailors at Dover moved to their action stations well before the outbreak of war. The Dover Patrol began operations at a strength of two destroyer flotillas – numbering some thirty ships – one of submarines, and many smaller craft, and they had a task of crucial importance in forming a shield to cover the passage of the BEF. The harbour was crammed and for ever astir with the comings and goings of dark ships of war.

In mid-September men of the Naval Division came through Dover en route for Antwerp, and their return in much reduced state, with 15,000 Belgian refugees, roused great alarm. Indeed, it extracted a plan for a massed exodus of Dover's people, in flocks across country as far as Ham Street (0033), where they were to entrain for the West. Then the front line became stabilised east of Dunkirk, and the people received no more than warning of the plan.

The Home Counties Division was released from its home defence duties in October and shipped to India, there to relieve regular battalions for service in France. Nevertheless fear of an invasion persisted. The Victorian forts by the Thames and Medway bristled with guns, new battery positions were constructed, and pillboxes were built. It is hard to identify any of them from their successors of 1940. At the same time there was great training activity, with the South-East reverting to its role in Roman times in reverse direction, that of forming a crucial link in the lines of communication. Even Richborough was revived as a transit port – or rather its name was adopted for what was really Stonar's harbour – and reinforcements flowed through Dover, Folkestone, and Newhaven as fast as the wounded arrived. All the Special Reserve battalions of the South-East regiments were stationed in East Kent, and as often before the Barham Downs was alive with military activity, excavations from which have often been attributed to Romans or Danes.

There was frequent harassment by the Germany Navy, beginning with a determined effort by submarines to penetrate Dover harbour early one morning in December 1914; it produced a thunder of fire from the guns on the piers and no certain loss to either side. Next came an air raid on the harbour, by two aeroplanes with two bombs, and on December 24 a single plane dropped a single bomb not far from Dover Castle, the first ever to land on British soil. It broke some windows and slightly injured a man by blast.

With the Dover Patrol much weakened by other demands, German destroyers indulged at night in some wild and practically harmless shelling of the coast in 1917. Margate and Broadstairs were their first targets, and Ramsgate subsequently received many shells. Dover's turn came on the night of April 20-21. About a hundred shells were haphazardly pumped in over a wide, mainly rural area, without a single round in reply from the coastal guns. However, Commander Evans intercepted the Germans as they withdrew with his own destroyer *Broke* and one named *Swift.* They attacked with torpedoes and, by ramming and boarding, with cutlasses. They sank two of the German destroyers, seriously damaged three more, and returned to a great reception with 105 prisoners, twenty-eight enemy dead, and twenty-two of their own.

The greatest day for Dover was that of St George, April 23, 1918, in the first hour of which the Patrol, under the newly appointed and promoted Vice-Admiral Roger Keyes, smote and blocked the German submarine base at Zeebrugge. A landing was made under devastating fire by groups of sailors and marines from HMS *Vindictive*, an old cruiser with large funnels and special fittings for the assault. She duly returned to Dover, battered almost beyond recognition, and berthed at 8 a.m., hailed by siren call and cheers from every ship in harbour. In the words of a survivor, 'It upset us a bit', for the great majority of these on board were wounded, dying, or dead. A dour process of evacuation followed, on the completion of which 156 corpses lay in the Market Hall. It was a tragic day for Dover, whose people felt closely identified with their Patrol. Yet it was also a proud day, and there was great rejoicing when the award of eight VCs was announced. It has been commemorated annually ever since, with the tolling of a bell transferred from Zeebrugge to Dover Town Hall as a token of Belgian gratitude.

Elsewhere air raids brought the war nearest the people. The first bombs fell on London's East End from a Zeppelin airship on May 31, 1915, and periodic recurrences caused much suffering and great anger, until at last Lt Leefe Robinson provided Londoners with a view of a Zeppelin descending through the night sky in flames, having shot it from his Camel fighter. This was on the night of September 2, 1916, and on the 4th he was awarded the Victoria Cross, the first man to be decorated for action over Britain. This was followed by other successes against Zeppelins and a decline in their use.

Folkestone was the recipient of the opening of a new and more formidable German air offensive. It was undertaken in the full daylight of May 25, 1917, by twenty-three double-engined Gothas, which had left London untouched because of bad visibility and offloaded their bombs partly on Shorncliffe Camp and partly on the crowded shopping arcade of Tontine Street, Folkestone. Here they killed ninety-five people and injured 260, far the heaviest loss yet suffered in a single raid.

A fortnight later the more legitimate target of Sheerness was attacked, causing the loss of forty-five lives but little material damage and with the anti-aircraft gunners scoring the rare achievement of a plane brought down. Then on June 12 (1917) twenty Gothas dropped over four tons of bombs on London, hit Liverpool Street Station, and killed 162 people, including children at school, and injured 432, without loss to themselves. This roused a great sense of outrage and brought about a better co-ordinated defence, with fighter squadrons withdrawn from France to operate from Bekesbourne (TR 2055), Throwley (TQ 9855), Detling (7957), Biggin Hill (4160), and three aerodromes north-east of London, interspersed between belts of anti-aircraft guns. After two less destructive raids on London the Germans gave up their daylight raids and turned instead to night ones, using planes aptly named Giants. These occasionally caused heavy but isolated damage, as for instance when 131 naval ratings were killed in their barracks at Chatham by a single bomb, and they drove Londoners to the shelter of the underground railway in their thousands. But the combination of guns and fighters gained strength and efficiency, and by bringing six bombers to the earth or coastal waters of Kent on the night of May 20, 1918, they gained the South-East immunity from enemy projectiles for twenty-two years.

It would appear that the enemy had no hand in the worst disaster to strike Kent. Ever since 1767 some mills between Faversham and the Swale had been in Crown ownership with the function and title of the Royal Gunpowder Factory (as which it remained until 1932). Shortly after noon on Easter Sunday, April 2, 1916, part of it disintegrated with a terrible ripple of explosions, spread by mutual detonation. Although only a skeleton staff were on duty, surrounded by earthworks, 160 people were killed or died soon afterwards. Production continued.

The regiments meanwhile had been making a prodigious contribution to the defeat of Germany and Turkey. The Queen's expanded to thirty-one battalions, the East Surrey to eighteen, the Buffs to fourteen, the Royal West Kent to eighteen, the Royal Sussex to twenty-four, the Middlesex to forty-six, and the Royal Fusiliers to no less than sixty-five. Of these 216 battalions, 128 went to war and lost around 70,500 in killed, a large proportion in three New Army divisions, the 12th, 18th, and 24th, in which men of the South-East fought side by side in all the big battles from Loos onwards. The London Regiment provided a further three divisions, all engaged in the fearful fighting on the Western Front. Others fought and died with the Regular and Territorial divisions, the Yeomanry, the Royal Navy, the Royal Marines, and the Royal Flying Corps. They did so in the understandable belief that it was a war to end all wars.

Anderida

Chapter 18

UNDER FIRE

Although in a calmer and more sombre atmosphere, the same procedure followed the outbreak of war in 1939 as in 1914. The 10th and 12th Infantry Brigades again sailed with the BEF on departure from Shorncliffe and Dover, journeying to France via Southampton, and in April 1940 they were joined on the Belgian frontier by the 44th Home Counties Division, whose under-equipped and under-trained duplicate, the 12th Division, also went to France.

Action began on May 10, 1940, when Germany invaded Holland and Belgium. By May 22 the Air Component of the BEF had been forced out of their aerodromes in France and given succour at Hawkinge (TR 2139) and Bekesbourne (205552), whence they continued their supporting role. On the heights above Folkestone, Hawkinge was the nearest aerodrome to the French coast and therefore the most vulnerable to air or ground attack, and the maze of pillboxes, ammunition bays, and shelters that are still littered around it show what was done for its protection. On May 26 the Flag Officer Commanding Dover, Vice-Admiral Sir Bertram Ramsay, received orders to carry out Operation Dynamo, for the evacuation of the BEF. He did this from his headquarters beneath the Castle, a catacomb of vaults to which refinements were still being added to the initial tunnelling carried out under threat from the two Napoleons.

The evacuation from Dunkirk was completed on June 4, by which time 224,686 British troops and 141,445 of their allies had been brought to England; they included about one third of the infantry of the 44th Division, virtually none of the 12th. The great majority came in destroyers, disembarking at Dover and being at once whisked away by train to different parts of the country. Others came in the little boats, the fishing smacks, tugs, and pleasure steamers, which dauntlessly chugged to and fro across the Channel. At one time fifty-two such vessels were counted trying to find space to offload their cargoes of khaki at Margate. The first aid men, volunteers of the Civil Defence, did a tremendous job in bringing in the wounded, many of whom were naked and covered in oil and had to be carried in this slippery state across the boats that were nearer the jetty. Like others, Margate's lifeboat performed the hazardous duty of ferrying men from the beach of Dunkirk out to destroyers, and the 600 saved in this manner could be added to the 46,000 soldiers who passed through the town's reception service. Never before had civilians been able to give such aid to the soldiers, and this sowed the sense of involvement which would flower into defiance under the eloquence of Churchill.

The fact of the evacuation showed that the Royal Navy and Royal Air Force were masters of the Channel, and despite the losses they had suffered, they could provide a powerful shield behind which to clothe the naked Army. The Navy could also provide guns for coastal defence from a large stock retained from the Great War. Since mobilisation territorials of the Royal Artillery had been manning a meagre total of twenty-two guns, of calibre 6-inches or more, along the coast of Kent and Sussex, twelve of them split between Gravesend and Sheerness, eight at Dover, and two at Newhaven. Enough for an additional thirty-nine batteries, mostly of two 4-inch or 6-inch guns, were provided by a great feat of search and extraction, and by the end of August the great majority of them had been mounted on hastily built emplacements stretching from Shornmead Fort to Bognor Regis. The Royal Navy helped with the provision of crews until this great new commitment could be fully undertaken by the Royal Artillery, who had ancient pieces of their own to man, such as the heavy howitzer on prominent display in Dane John Gardens, Canterbury.

Dover's armament, on completion of the evacuation from Dunkirk, amounted to three elderly 9.2-inch guns behind the casemated earthworks of the Citadel Battery (see map on pages 16-17), three 6-inchers under the crude overhead cover of St Martin's Battery, which is still in conspicuous view from the harbour, two more 6-inchers in Langdon Battery, covering the Eastern Arm, and a further two on the Pier Turret, above the giants stored in grease since 1902. Two pairs of twin 6-pounders and a quick-firing 12-pounder were mounted on other parts of the harbour's arms, backed by twelve searchlights, and embrasures for other light guns can be seen on the Castle's eastern wall. None of these weapons had the range to do more than repel an attack, and visiting Dover with the knowledge that the Germans were constructing emplacements for siege guns that could easily strike Dover, Churchill seethed with the urge to strike back. Again the Navy came to his aid. Two 14-inchers were made available, but one needed much more work on its modernisation than the other. A battery of Royal Marines was formed to man them.

The site chosen for the first of these guns, which was named Winnie after its founder, was on the seawards slope of a valley, west of St Margaret's and a good two miles north-east of Dover. Nearly two miles of railway line was laid to bring it from Martin Mill Station (3446) and a great concrete platform was built for it, together with magazines and posts for fire control, which were dug and cemented into the hillside. The work was completed by the end of July, and Winnie was duly installed beneath an acre of camouflage netting. The gunners had the protection only of the shield attached to the gun and of some earthen mounds. Concrete to the height of a bungalow was being set as overhead protection for their foe.

The first shells from a German battery whizzed across the Channel on August 12, landing on the west side of Dover, where they inflicted some casualties. Winnie made first response on August 22, not at the German guns, but at its primary target, shipping. The result proved the need for further practice, and while the practice brought improvement it in turn proved that guns of this size could not withstand more than occasional bursts of fire, because of the tremendous strain on their barrels. However, Winnie could at least give veracity to the claim that fire was being returned and thus raise the morale of the British people. It also served to divert the enemy's fire from Dover town onto itself. But the people of Dover showed no gratitude. They were angered by misleading reports of 'artillery duels' and attributed everything that fell among themselves to provocation by the British guns, of which Winnie was for six months the only active competitor.

A complementary project, which also owed much to the drive and imagination of Churchill, was the provision of guns permanently mounted on long railway trucks, most of them refurbished veterans of the Great War. Twenty-seven of them eventually arrived in Kent, three of them to be manned by Royal Marines on the line running northwards from Guston tunnel, north of Dover, where they received their quota of enemy shells. The remainder were manned by the 2nd and 3rd Super Heavy Regiments, RA, and had the task of blasting any beach on which the enemy might land and any lodgement he might make. The shells from their 10-inch howitzers or 9.2-inch guns had tremendous capacity for destruction, but the inevitable ban on registering targets by gunfire would of course have hampered their accuracy, and their rate of fire could never have been higher than slow.

The first battery arrived early in September and deployed one gun in a siding at Folkestone, the other at Hythe, and the former became the only one of the two regiments ever to record the firing of a shot, at a far distant naval craft. Its recoil knocked it off its rails. Nestled in cuttings and tunnels, with hidden engines available to give them mobility, other batteries were positioned at Shepherdswell (6966) and at Eythorne (7267), north of Dover, and others had guns dotted among sidings on either side of that great repair centre, Ashford. The last to arrive, in February 1941, was a giant 18-incher named Bochebuster. It was placed in the Bishopsbourne tunnel on the now defunct Canterbury-Elham line.

The 1st London (later 56th) Division were the only field troops in the South-East prior to Dunkirk, and in May they were joined by the 45th, who belonged to and came from the West Country. They were assigned to the defence of the ports and the elimination of parachutists, the 1st London being spread from Margate to Folkestone and the 45th from Rye to Bognor with special emphasis on Newhaven. To improve their meagre prospects of repulsing the enemy, scaffolding had been erected at speed along the beach and pillboxes had been built, both by a large force of civilian workers under contract, and belts of wire and mines were laid by itinerant groups of Sappers and Pioneers. Yet these divisions had barely a third of their complement of field guns and machine-guns with which to cover their huge frontages, and had only six anti-tank guns between the two of them. Priority had been given to the re-equipment of the veteran divisions returned from Dunkirk, and the bulk of them were held in reserve on either side of London, waiting to halt the enemy on an inner ring of defences covering the essential production centres of Britain. In the South-East it was based on the North Downs, as far as but exclusive of Maidstone, and it extended little beyond the line chosen for that of the Volunteers' forts following the *Battle of Dorking* controversy. Once the forward divisions had failed in their attempts to stop the Germans gaining sizable bridgeheads, they were to fall back on this line through stop positions offering prospect of delay on the various riverlines.

Such was the plan of Britain's senior general, Sir Edmund Ironside, who had been transferred from the post of CIGS to that of C-in-C Home Forces even before the evacuation from Dunkirk was complete and had his headquarters in Hammersmith. The old forts had been built while he was coming of age, and he must have rued their return to civilian ownership. Now gaps were cut through the railings and brambles that surrounded them, and earnest examination was made of their casemates and mountings. That of Box Hill had suddenly ceased to be 'the idlest monument of a whim', as it had been described by a wandering writer, Eric Parker, in 1935.

The forward defences of this line ran along the Rivers Eden and Medway, and as many pillboxes and the triangular anti-tank slabs known as dragon's teeth can be seen on their northern banks, particularly around Edenbridge and Tonbridge, as on the North Downs themselves. The pillboxes vary enormously in their prominence. Some are absurdly conspicuous, indicating the haste with which they were built and poor liaison between contractors and military commanders, the latter of whom were often the mere agents of the unknown troops to whom the duty of occupation would fall. Most of the pillboxes are hexagonal in shape, capable of mounting two machine-guns, and all the early ones lacked the strength of concrete to withstand a shell from the 37-mm anti-tank gun with which German formations were equipped on a lavish scale.

Although based on a realistic assessment of his troops' capability, and on the importance of defence in depth, Ironside's plan was too defeatist to retain Churchill's approval, and on July 20 Sir Alan Brooke became C-in-C in his place. Instead of merely causing delay, the forward divisions now had the task of driving the enemy back, and they began to receive the equipment to achieve this. Much had already been done to make their areas defensible, and most modern relics to be found on famous sites may well be those of Ironside's regime, such as the concrete blocks by the battlefield of Hastings (749158), the pillboxes fitted inside Pevensey's Anderida Castle, the one by Bodiam Castle, covering the bridge over the Rother, the extension of the double-Martello Dymchurch Redoubt (129321), and the dragon's teeth on the northern side of Dover Castle. The most impressive monument to the spirit of those times is the Admiralty Citadel in London, overlooking Horse Guards Square and with field of fire covering The Mall. Any thought of concealment here appears to have been spurned in favour of providing a symbol of the Government's determination to stay in position and fight it out.

As part of the far spread Eastern Command, whose headquarters were at Hounslow, the newly formed 12th Corps undertook responsibility for Kent and Sussex, and a large part of Surrey too, exercised from an underground headquarters in the south-west outskirts of Tunbridge Wells (575375). Its GOC was a Grenadier, Lt-Gen Andrew Thorne, who had commanded about the hardest fought division in the retreat to Dunkirk, the 48th. He was determined, above all else, to deny the Germans the chance to rampage unchecked that they had enjoyed in France, and he allotted a co-ordinated part to every static unit, whether training or administrative, and to every unit of the Home Guard, as the Local Defence Volunteers had been renamed by Churchill. Kent and Sussex are both dotted with villages lying in enclosed, choppy country, and each offered excellent facilities for defence. To prevent the roads being blocked by refugees – and thus remove a nightmare of the campaign in France – orders were issued by the Government for the evacuation from the coastal sector of all persons not engaged on essential work, and those who remained were urged to stay at home if the enemy landed. Signposts were removed to deprive the enemy of their aid, and church bells were to pass their warnings as of old, but only of a landing from the sky.

The Home Guard filled the role of the old part-time Volunteers, with the big difference that they included many men of no great age who had gained immense battle experience in the Great War. Practically every town and every rural district had its own battalion affiliated to and wearing the badge of its county regiment – those wearing that of the Royal West Kent (as in the television series, 'Dad's Army') rose to a total of thirty-eight – and once armed with a British or American rifle, as most were by the end of August, they could undoubtedly have imposed a great impediment on the enemy's advance. Their special art was to ambush tanks in villages and set them alight by use of petrol bombs or 'Molotov cocktails'. Plans were also made to ignite flame traps along stretches of road by the pumping of petrol, as on the defile of Lydden Hill on the Canterbury-Dover road.

The Deneholes reverted to the clandestine usage of their legendary origin. Together with others newly constructed, these deep old shafts formed the hide-outs of the civilians who bravely volunteered to harass the Germans by sabotage if their land were invaded. These men were carefully picked by Thorne's fellow Grenadier, the author Peter Fleming, under cover of forming the Corps Observation Unit. Their largest base was in King's Wood, near the pilgrims' route to Canterbury (0350), where a hide for 120 men was constructed beneath a strange boat-shaped depression that had been made to hold an airship in the Great War, from which to make flights in search of submarines. The resistance men were at first called 'stay-behind parties' and subsequently Auxiliary Units, on expansion under War Office direction. They were made part of the Home Guard but had to keep their duties secret from the main part.

From August 8 there was a great and sustained increase in enemy air activity, combined with the shelling of Dover, and at times of Ramsgate and Folkestone too. The aerodromes in the South-East were divided into four sectors under command of No 11 Fighter Group, as exercised from Uxbridge by Air Vice-Marshal Park. The Hornchurch Sector operated with three squadrons from Essex, each of an intended twelve aircraft, and it had a fourth flying long-range Blenheim fighters from Manston (near Ramsgate, 3366). Biggin Hill (in the extreme west of Kent, 4160) itself had a Spitfire and a Hurricane squadron and controlled another of Hurricanes at Hawkinge and one of Blenheims at Gravesend (6672). Kenley (some 5 miles west of Biggin Hill, 3357) housed two fighter squadrons and controlled a third at Croydon (3163, and like Gravesend and Kenley aerodromes, no longer there). Tangmere (near Chichester, 9107) was the only aerodrome of importance in Sussex, and it had three squadrons of Hurricanes. Park had a further two squadrons at Northolt, on the north-west side of London, and three in Hampshire. Their hour had come.

It was an extraordinary experience for the civilian neighbours of the pilots to observe the complex smoke-chains of aerial battle and to pray for the success and indeed lives of men with whom they were in daily contact. There was a tremendous feeling of participation, with so many people combining essential work in field, factory, or office with duty in the Home Guard — who were usually the first to reach a fallen plane or pilot — the Observer Corps, Air Raid Precautions, Police, Fire, and Ambulance services. The sun also played its part, with long periods of brilliance, in sustaining morale.

The Luftwaffe struck some deadly blows, most of all on Tangmere, which in a raid on August 16 lost almost half its aircraft. By the end of August both Hawkinge and Manston had been so heavily pounded that they were kept open only as emergency landing grounds, their squadrons withdrawn. Biggin Hill suffered so heavily in the three days of August 30-September 1 that its squadrons, newly raised to three, were reduced to one. Then the Germans, miraculously, turned to other targets, among them such aerodromes of lesser importance as Lympne (TR 1135), West Malling (TQ 6555), Detling (808590), which was now used by Coastal Command, and that birthplace of flying in England, Eastchurch (9871). They then concentrated on London, culminating with a massive attack on September 15, in which the Luftwaffe lost sixty planes — a number reported by the British as 185 from the claims made by pilots – and the RAF twenty-six. Although less overwhelming than supposed, this was indeed the decisive victory of the Battle of Britain, and the rejoicing was justified.

Expectation of invasion had reached its peak a week earlier, based on observation of the assembly of barges in the Channel ports. Indeed the codeword to stand to, Cromwell, was issued on the evening of Saturday, September 7, and this led to such a pealing of church bells to summon the Home Guard that Brooke ordered that in future they must only be rung on the authority of a witness of the descent of at least twenty-five parachutists. The issue of Cromwell was in fact a trifle premature, for the revised date planned for the landing (Operation Sea Lion) was at dawn on September 22. It was to be made by nine divisions coming from as far apart as Rotterdam and Le Havre in 1,722 barges, 155 larger transports, and 471 tugs; two were to land between Folkestone and Dungeness (both exclusive), two opposite Rye and east of Hastings, two at Bexhill and Pevensey, and three at and on either side of Newhaven. In addition the 7th Parachute Division was to land on the high ground about Lympne, and the 22nd Air Landing Division was in reserve, awaiting the capture of Lympne aerodrome. Two hundred and fifty tanks were to accompany the assault divisions.

To oppose these eleven divisions, Thorne now had the equivalent of four, not counting his static troops, with a further two, including armour, available for quick release from GHQ reserve. He had also had his frontage reduced, being relieved of that part of Sussex west of the Arun, and he had entrusted his right flank to the 1st Motorised Machine Gun Brigade, covering the sweeps of the Downs above Brighton and Shoreham, a zone outside the intended landing. The 45th Division were installed from Newhaven to Rye, the objective of seven divisions, and the only reserve immediately available was the 29th Brigade, of four regular battalions returned from overseas. The 7th Corps, in GHQ reserve, was well placed to join the battle here, being grouped around East Grinstead and Reigate. It was the most powerful striking force Brooke had, consisting of the 1st Army Tank Brigade and the 1st Armoured Division, who together could muster some 250 tanks, half of them medium or cruiser and half light tanks, and the redoubtable 1st Canadian Division. They could have made the Germans' capture and retention of Newhaven no certainty.

In Kent the 1st London Division had received a fourth brigade, which was positioned north of Ashford. Like Moore before him, Thorne was concerned about the Romney Marsh. Two spies were captured at Hythe and two at Dungeness on September 3-4, both pairs having sneaked in by sea, which was worrying. Thorne had made plans for a partial flooding of the marsh by breaching the sea wall. He had been promised another regular brigade, and he was placing it behind the canal between Rye and Aldington, but it would have arrived too late to disrupt the combined sea and air landings if they had met their schedule. However, two commandos were available for immediate counter-attack, and in reserve south of Maidstone Thorne had a division of high offensive potential, the New Zealand. Good depot troops could also be summoned from Ashford, Shorncliffe,

Canterbury, Maidstone, and Chatham. The German paras would have been guaranteed a hard fight.

Obviously all depended on the ability of the seaborne troops to arrive. As their Naval C-in-C, Admiral von Raeder, well realised, their prospects were bleak. His entire battle strength had been reduced to three cruisers and four destroyers, mainly by losses in Norwegian waters, when he made his plans at the start of July, and there appears to have been very little increase since. He had little faith in the efficacy of minefields for flank protection and had to rely primarily on the nightly ten hours of darkness as shield for the tugs that had each to pull their four or five river barges at a maximum speed of four knots for distances that in some cases well exceeded 100 miles, necessitating a daylight start. The slightest swell would have upset them, and few of their pilots had experience of navigation at sea.

The Royal Air Force had been bombing concentrations of barges since September 5, with results that proved that the Luftwaffe could have done little to impede the flow of British warships from their ports; some ten per cent of the transports were disabled in a fortnight's bombing. The Auxiliary Patrol formed the Royal Navy's antennae, providing a thick screen of little vessels, including trawlers and drifters, able to summon more powerful ships to disrupt minelaying and intercept hostile convoys, of whose coming radar would provide earliest warning. It was a drawback that none except a few motor torpedo boats could come from Dover, for its port was considered so vulnerable that its destroyer flotilla had been withdrawn.

Nore Command (according to the Admiralty location list on September 30) had two cruisers, nine destroyers, two sloops, and five MTBs based on Sheerness and Chatham, and seven destroyers and seventeen smaller fighting craft based on Harwich, all within two hours' sail (at 30 knots) of the eastern part of the enemy's objective. Mountbatten's flotilla of nine destroyers, plus two cruisers, were waiting in the Humber, also under Nore Command, and could reach the battle zone within seven hours of sailing. The Home Fleet's main striking force of five battleships, with cruiser and destroyer escorts, would have come in from Scottish ports to dominate the North Sea, unaware that the Germans had nothing worthy of their calibre in fit state to fight them.

Portsmouth Command could deploy one cruiser, seventeen destroyers, and six smaller craft, admirably placed to smash the transports bringing three divisions from Le Havre, and from Plymouth, at six hours' sail from the objectives, Western Approaches Command could despatch one battleship, two cruisers, and ten destroyers. In all, seven cruisers and fifty-two destroyers were thus within easy range to intervene within twelve hours of receiving notice, and their retention in home waters imposed heavy loss on the convoys they might have escorted, a peril eased by the receipt of fifty old American destroyers in October.

Fully alive to the tradition of Drake, the captains of all craft were primed to close on the enemy and 'burn, sink, destroy'. Again, there was a plan to send fireships into the Channel ports, and if nothing else they would have illuminated targets for the RAF. There were also plans, of both naval and army designing, for laying walls of flaming oil across the sea, but these would probably have been less effective than rumours of charred German corpses led people to expect. As for the destroyers, their biggest problem would have been to depress their 4.5-inch guns to hit the barges at short range. Many had acquired Bren light-machine-guns during the evacuation from Dunkirk and kept them ready for close quarter work.

As was agreed by both sides, at a study held at Camberley in 1974 between teams of experienced German and British officers, some of the assault troops might have arrived across a sea that happened to be calm on the chosen night, but they had no chance of retaining their bridgehead without the degree of air supremacy deemed necessary by Raeder from the start. Since it was made clear on September 15 that the Luftwaffe had emphatically failed to achieve the domination required, Hitler had no option but to call off the venture, at least until the following spring.

He turned instead to demoralising the people of London, and on every night of the next two months, with only one exception, the bombs were poured upon them, the total according to German records amounting to 13,651 tons of high explosive and 12,586 incendiaries, as delivered between September 7 and November 13 by 11,117 aircraft-runs. Their failure to break the spirit of the Londoners was crucial to the result of the war and was due to their magnificent pluck and to the shelter provided by the underground railway.

The anti-aircraft guns could do little against the night bomber except fortify the people by the sound of their firing. Reinforcements brought the total of heavy guns about London to 235, and they belched away from such open places as Hyde Park. There were also heavy concentrations of guns around the mouth of the Medway, and certainly they deterred daylight raids on shipping and shipways with aid from barrage balloons: a good memorial to them can be seen north of the Medway at about 803755 in the concrete emplacements of a troop of four 3.7-inch guns. Offshore from this area great loss to shipping and great anxiety were caused by the dropping of magnetic mines, which would lie on the seabed until attracted by a ship. The only way to counter this menace was to erect fortresses out at sea, armed with Bofors and 3.7-inch AA guns. Eight were constructed and towed out to be installed on stands of concrete. The Army manned three in shallow waters, Nore Tower (off Sheppey) and two off Shoeburyness, Red Sands and Shivering Sands, and the Navy had forts of a different type, mounting three decks made of steel, further out to sea. Six remain, a number recently reduced from seven to deprive a broadcaster of his pirate lair.

In February 1941 the South-East was turned into a separate military command and entrusted to a fine trainer of troops, Lt-Gen Bernard Paget, with headquarters at Reigate. In May Thorne was promoted to Scottish Command and handed over 12th Corps to the future Field Marshal Montgomery, and it is mark of the Army's growth that he was responsible for the defence only of Kent and had three divisions, including the 44th Home Counties, and two independent brigades for this purpose. On June 22 Hitler indicated, in the manner of Napoleon, that he had turned his back on the Channel by launching his invasion of Russia, and the officers and men of 12th Corps might have relaxed if they had had any other GOC.

Throughout 1941 guns kept arriving in the vicinity of Dover with the range to smite the German ships that hugged the French coast. Winnie's partner, Pooh, was installed in February, on the other side of St Margaret's, and was followed by guns of the newly formed 540 Coast Regiment, RA, positioned between Winnie and the shore, four 9.2-inchers forming the South Foreland batteries and three 6-inchers that of Fan Bay. On the other side of Dover 520 Coast Regiment established three 8-inchers east of Hougham (292396), three 6-inchers on the cliff's edge of Lydden Spout (284389), and three 8-inchers perched above Folkestone next Capel (242379). With the aid of radar, and of spotter planes from Manston, the gunners claimed an ever increasing number of hits, in daylight and more often at night.

They therefore felt deep chagrin when the trio of warships, *Scharnhorst, Gneisenau,* and *Prinz Eugen,* made passage of the Straits when bound from Brest to Kiel on the foggy morning of February 11, 1942. The jamming of the Fairlight radar station obstructed warning of their coming and deprived the batteries west of Dover of their chance. The Royal Marines had hastily to be summoned from training, and only the South Foreland batteries' 9.2-inchers let fly with any hope of success. They claimed three hits on *Scharnhorst* but could not confirm them. Air attacks included a most gallant one by six slow torpedo-armed Swordfish aircraft of the Fleet Air Arm from Manston. None returned.

Within three months 540 Coast Regiment received the most powerful reinforcements ever granted to the Army, two 15-inch guns that had been made for the defence of Singapore. Emplacements for them, and all the necessary ancillary constructions, some of which are still on view, were built near the South Foreland batteries in front of Wanstone Farm, which continued to carry out its agricultural function. The great eruptions around it brought the eventual total of ships claimed to have been sunk by all the coastal guns, after investigation by aircraft, to twenty-six.

The Germans had over fifty guns of calibre ranging from 150-406-mm encased in concrete between Calais and Boulogne, and with command of the air lost, and in fear that the invasion of Normandy was merely a ruse before that of the Pas de Calais, they hit Dover ever more frequently, ever more indiscriminately. The protests of its unfortunate inhabitants grew ever more strident, made in the still persistent belief that they were victims of a wanton artillery duel. Not until September 1944 were Dover's guns at last aimed at the German batteries, and they now gave covering fire for the land advance by the 2nd Canadian Corps. They fired 532 rounds and claimed forty-two direct hits, although doing little more than denting the great emplacements, as examination proved. By September 30 the Canadians had captured Calais and all the battery positions, and quiet at last descended on 'Hell-Fire Corner', as journalists had christened it.

Certainly the nickname was merited. Seven hundred bombs, 2,260 shells, two parachute mines, and three flying bombs are recorded as having fallen on the town, completely destroying 957 houses and making a further 1,936 uninhabitable. Yet out of a population reduced by evacuation from 40,000 to 16,000, only 212 civilians lost their lives, together with 283 servicemen. Not one of the guns had been knocked out beyond repair. Dover had lived up to its reputation of being tough of hide.

It was appropriate that the gunners of Dover should have been able to give fire support to the 2nd Canadian Corps, for it had been stationed in the area at the time of the Normandy landing, as part of the successful cover plan. Newhaven played its part in the real operation, being the point of departure of the left assault division, the 3rd British, and Richborough sent out a portion of the Mulberry Harbour. About the largest concentration of troops, near 5,000, was made at Bushy Park, on the north bank of the Thames due west of Kingston. Here General Eisenhower housed his Supreme Headquarters until taking it to Normandy in July.

London in 1940 and 1941, Canterbury in 1942, Eastbourne, Hastings, Brighton, and Margate in 1943, and London again heavily in the early months of 1944 all received particularly savage visitations from the Luftwaffe, and now in June 1944, after the start of the invasion, a new form of torment was inflicted on the people in the shape of the flying bomb, or 'doodlebug'. London was as usual the main recipient, and in the course of three months 2,419 fell in its region, despite the destruction of 3,463 by AA guns and by new RAF Typhoon fighters using aerodromes on the Romney Marsh such as Brenzett (0128), New Romney (0526), and Lydd (0623) that had initially served as emergency landing fields and been developed for use by American fighters covering the invasion of Europe. Probably the heaviest military loss was caused by a direct hit on the Guards' Chapel at Wellington Barracks during Sunday church parade. After the launching sites of the flying bombs had been captured, the Germans opened up with long-range rockets, and when the last of these terrifying missiles landed, on March 27, 1945, the total counted upon London reached 517. Of the 146,777 civilian casualties (killed or seriously injured) suffered in Britain throughout the war, 80,397 were incurred in the London area, of which nearly 30,000 were from flying bombs or rockets.

It was a battered land to which the troops returned from their widespread travels, which for the 44th Division ended with dispersal in Egypt after El Alamein and for the 1st London or 56th, as also for many other troops from the South-East, with the capitulation of the enemy in Italy. The regiments suffered far fewer casualties than in the Great War, and this made some amends for the heavy loss on the home front.

Shornmead

Chapter 19

DEFENCES DISMANTLED

It is impossible for the layman to know how effectively guided missiles, from ground, sea, or air, can carry out the task formerly assigned to guns. Certainly the trust placed in them appeared to speed the erosion of defences that follows every war. Its first effect was the disbandment in 1954 of Anti-Aircraft Command, to which the South-East contributed some twelve recently reconstituted territorial regiments, who had played a great part in the recent war. From the historical viewpoint, worse followed at the close of 1956, when the territorial coast regiments were disbanded, thus denuding the shore of its guns for the first time since Henry VIII had awoken to the urgent need to provide them.

Two regiments were involved in the South-East, both newly reorganised: 410 (Kent) Coast Regiment and the descendant of the Gravesend Volunteer Artillery, 415 (Thames and Medway) Coast Regiment, and because it was the easiest way to remove them, the men had the mortification of watching their beloved guns sliced into pieces by acetylene cutters. Their emplacements became tattered remains, often adjacent to older vintages of fortification, such as casemates, loopholed walls, and revetted earthworks. The connoisseur can find a fine collection, preserved by order, along the 1,000 yards of seafront stretching eastwards from Garrison Point, Sheerness, part of it on the premises of the Medway Ports Authorities. There are no visible means of deterring any raider who might wish to emulate the Dutch. But the decline of Chatham in naval importance reduces the incentive.

At Dover, the three huge aerials above Langdon Bay at least convey the impression that a sentry still stands alert. Moreover, Dover still has a battalion of regular infantry, living in Connaught Barracks, adjacent to the Castle and under the eye of the Garrison Commander from his living quarters in the Constable's Tower. Nearby the sons of soldiers are educated at the Duke of York's Royal Military School, and at the comparatively new Old Park Barracks (3044) is the Junior Leaders Regiment, Royal Engineers. But elsewhere the remains of military activity conjure their ghosts, and nowhere do they intrude more nostalgically than on the slopes, luxuriant with weed and wild flower, of the Western Heights. Certainly the harbour throbs with activity, but not with ships of the Royal Navy, who gave up their base there in 1919.

The erosion of the Infantry began in 1947, with orders reducing every regiment to a single battalion, and it continued with the suspension of national service, ordered in 1957. This brought about the amalgamation of Surrey's two regiments into The Queen's Royal Surrey Regiment and that of Kent's two to form The Queen's Own Buffs, The Royal Kent Regiment. It also brought the transfer of the Royal Fusiliers to the newly formed Fusilier Brigade and the formation of a central depot for the four survivors of the Home Counties Brigade. The one chosen was the new one built for the Buffs and named Howe Barracks, Canterbury, after their wartime depot commander. It stands on a hill overlooking the Cathedral.

It was the hope of the War Office that the Colonels of Regiments within each brigade would opt to convert it to a large regiment, thus forming an organisation less vulnerable to the continuing demands of reduction and expediency. The four Home Counties Colonels were in due course unanimously persuaded, and on the last day of 1966 The Queen's Regiment came into being, with four regular battalions representing the former regiments of Surrey, Kent, Sussex, and Middlesex. Almost at once a further reorganisation was ordered under which depots were to be grouped on a divisional basis. Depot The Queen's was moved to Bassingbourn, in Cambridgeshire, leaving only the civilian-staffed Regimental Headquarters at Canterbury, in barracks filled on occasions by a regular battalion. The Royal Regiment of Fusiliers is also served by the divisional depot at Bassingbourn. Thus not one of the seven thriving depots of the South-East's county regiments is left. The eighteen regular battalions they once served have been reduced (with the inclusion of one of Fusiliers) to four, for the 4th Queen's were obliged to give up a long struggle for survival in 1973. The remaining three do their best to keep alive the traditions of six old regiments.

Happily, the spirit of Sir John Moore is kept alive at Shorncliffe by the Infantry Junior Leaders Regiment, who occupy barracks named after him. The Guards Depot continues to prosper in Surrey, now at Pirbright, north of Guildford, to which it moved in 1960, having left its barracks at Caterham to be modernised for use by a battalion; the Foot Guards have suffered reduction only from ten to eight battalions. The Royal Artillery, Royal Engineers, and Royal Marines continue to maintain thriving strongholds respectively at Woolwich, Chatham, and Deal; they too have suffered reduction on a smaller scale than the Infantry of the Line. At Ashford, Kent, a rare advance has been made by the military with the arrival there of the Intelligence Corps Centre and Depot, from Maresfield, Sussex.

The Territorial Army has suffered some crippling blows, the worst coming in 1965, with its virtual disbandment in its old form and reorganisation as a mere reinforcement corps. However, the determination of its members to keep it in being has proved stronger than that of impecunious governments bent on suppressing it. There has been a revival since 1970. Thus the TA strength of the new Queen's Regiment, having sunk to a single battalion out of a total of seven on the strength of the founder regiments at the time of the amalgamation, now stands at two battalions, both with most important parts to play on mobilisation. All those of the London Regiment have long since been absorbed within the framework of regiments of the Regular Army, eleven with transfer to the Royal Artillery, and some continue to play active parts. The Artists Rifles became the 21 Special Air Service. The eight Yeomanry regiments have been reduced to mere components of the Royal Yeomanry. Only the Honourable Artillery Company serves on untouched, in title, strength, and tradition.

It was a strange anomoly of the 1965 reorganisation that the title of Volunteer was revived for those battalions assigned important roles, whereas those sentenced to slide into limbo retained the title Territorial. The Volunteer battalions should have been named Special Reserve, for they filled the role assigned the converted Militia in 1908, that of reinforcing regular battalions. Their role has been changed to one of greater independence, restoring validity to the title Territorial Army. Yet they remain Volunteer battalions.

Just as the Army consists of a mixture of the old and the new, with the one intruding on the other as much in the choice of titles as in the ritual of parade, so the remains of fortifications convey the same sense of timelessness. One of the best examples can be seen from the main road between Rye and Winchelsea: a 1940 pillbox covers the road itself; the gaunt hulk of a Tudor castle stands close behind it; beyond is a Martello tower; and the 13th Century Ypres Tower commands entry into Rye itself. There is a span of seven hundred years between these crops, and yet they have more in common than in contrast.

For even closer converging of the centuries a look at Anderida or Pevensey Castle is recommended from the car park on its east side. It will be observed that the Normans merged their castle into the Roman wall here and that five slits have been carved through it, for defence in 1940. It has had an extraordinary motley of defenders: foreign mercenaries of Rome, waiting to lay harsh hand on raiding pirates and regarding the fort as just one more station in a long itinerary; a forlorn remnant of Britons, ill equipped to withstand assault by the Saxons, who would kill them all; swashbuckling Norman knights, thrilled to have arrived on English soil; the proud Bishop Odo and his brother Robert, squeezed into capitulation in a six weeks' siege; peasant soldiers of Edward III, wary of fearsome invaders from France; flamboyant Elizabethans, mounting cannon on the crumbling castle, with an eye on the heights of Beachy Head for signal of the Armada's coming; stern soldiers of Cromwell, with knowledge that Van Tromp had gained victory in the Channel; scarlet-clad militiamen, awaiting completion of the Martello towers on the nearby beach; khaki-clad territorials of the 45th West Country Division, casting an appreciative eye on the constructional refinements that turned the ancient monument into a modern redoubt and an enthralled eye towards the sky, where the fate of their country was being decided; and later in this same war, American airmen in fur-lined jackets, manning a radar set. Who, one wonders, will be the next?

Appendix

BOOKS CONSULTED

GENERAL

Winston S. Churchill: *A History of The English-Speaking Peoples* (Cassell, four volumes, 1956-58)
Victoria History of Kent
Victoria History of Surrey
Ronald Jessup: *South-East England* (Thames & Hudson, 1970)
Frank Jessup: *A History of Kent* (Darwen Finlayson, 1958)
J.R. Armstrong: *A History of Sussex* (Darwen Finlayson, 1961)
J. Bavington Jones: *Annals of Dover* (Dover Express, 1916)
Rivers Scott: *The Gateway of England* (Dover Harbour Board, 1956)

ROMAN PERIOD

Julius Caesar: *The Gallic War,* translated by H.J. Edwards (Heinemann, 1963)
Sheppard Frere: *Britannia* (Routledge & Kegan Paul, 1967)
Graham Webster & Donald R. Dudley: *The Roman Conquest of Britain* (Batsford, 1965)
Graham Webster: *The Roman Imperial Army* (Black, 1969)

FROM SAXON TO TUDOR TIMES

The Anglo-Saxon Chronicle, translated by G.N. Garmonsway (Dent, 1954)
Sir Frank Stenton: *Anglo-Saxon England* (Oxford University Press, 1971)
R.H. Hodgkin: *A History of The Anglo-Saxons* (Oxford University Press, 1952)
Henry S. Chapman: *The Story of Dula* (Newnes, 1921)
C.H. Lemmon: *The Field of Hastings* (Rudd & Gillatt, 1957) – quotes original sources
W. Douglas Simpson: *Castles in England and Wales* (Batsford, 1969)
Hilary Turner: *Town Defences in England and Wales* (John Baker, 1971)
Barbara Willard: *Chichester and Lewes* (Longman, Young, 1970)
Tufton Beamish: *Battle Royal* (Muller, 1965)

17th CENTURY

C.R. Butt: *Surrey and The Civil War* (Army Historical Research)
Charles Thomas-Stanford: *Sussex in The Great Civil War* (Chiswick Press, 1910)
H.F. Abell: *Kent and The Great Civil War* (Kentish Express, 1901)
Alan Everitt: *The Community of Kent and The Great Rebellion* (Leicester University Press, 1966)

J.M. Russell: *The History of Maidstone* (1881, republished by John Hallewell, 1978) – quotes Fairfax's despatch on Battle of Maidstone
Brig. O.F.G. Hogg: *The Royal Arsenal* (Oxford University Press, 1963)
Jock Haswell: *James II: Soldier and Sailor* (Hamish Hamilton, 1972)

18th to 20th CENTURY

J.R. Western: *The English Militia in the Eighteenth Century* (Routledge & Kegan Paul, 1965)
Carola Oman: *Sir John Moore* (Hodder & Stoughton, 1953)
P.A.L. Vine: *The Royal Military Canal* (David & Charles, 1972)
Sheila Sutcliffe: *Martello Towers* (David & Charles, 1972)
Brig J.R.E. Hamilton-Baillie: *Fixed Fortifications of Chatham* (R.E. Journal, March, 1974)
Col. K.W. Maurice-Jones: *The History of Coast Artillery in The British Army* (R.A. Institution, 1959)
Maj-Gen C.S. Akers: *Defences of Dover* (Professional Papers, R.E., 1886)
I.V. Hogg: *Coastal Defences of England and Wales 1856-1956* (David & Charles, 1974)
Dover and The European War, 1914-18 (Dover Express)
Philip Warner: *The Zeebrugge Raid* (Kimber, 1978)
Full Record of Raids (Thanet Advertiser, 1919)
Basil Collier: *Defence of The United Kingdom* (H.M.S.O., 1957)
F.K. Mason: *Battle Over Britain* (McWhirter, 1969)
David Lampe: *The Last Ditch* (Cassell, 1968)
Ronald Wheatley: *Operation Sea Lion* (Clarendon Press, 1958)
John Reed: *The Cross-Channel Guns* (Battle of Britain Prints, 1980) – gives detailed deployment of all batteries.
Peter Fleming: *Invasion 1940* (Hart-Davis, 1957)

INDEX